NONE *Shall Be* BARREN

A complete armor for breaking every yoke of infertility

PROPHETESS NONNIE ROBERSON

NONE SHALL BE BARREN – A complete armor for breaking every yoke of infertility

Copyright© 2017 by Prophetess Nonnie Roberson

nonnier@gmail.com

All rights reserved. No part of this book may be reproduced or transmitted by any means - electronic, mechanical, digital, photocopying, recording or by any information storage or retrieval system, except by the copyright holder's written permission.

This excludes adaptation for religious/educational purposes and brief excerpts/reviews in Newspapers, Newsletters, Magazines and journals

TABLE OF CONTENTS

DEDICATION 5

ACKNOWLEDGEMENT 7

PREFACE 9

SECTION A 13

BARRENNESS IS NOT OF GOD 13

CHAPTER ONE 15

CHAPTER TWO 23

CHAPTER THREE 31

CHAPTER FOUR 40

CHAPTER FIVE 47

CHAPTER SIX 57

SECTION B 65

FIGHT FOR YOUR FRUITFULNESS 65

CHAPTER SEVEN 66

CHAPTER EIGHT 77

CHAPTER NINE 91

CHAPTER TEN 105

MORE TESTIMONIES TO BOOST YOUR FAITH 118

ABOUT THE AUTHOR 134

DEDICATION

I dedicate this book to God the Father, God the Son and God the Holy Spirit, for the divine unction and grace to do the work of ministry.

To every woman and every family believing God for the fruit of the womb. As you prayerfully read this book, with faith, may the unusual grace for fruitfulness on my life and in this book, launch you to unprecedented fruitfulness in Jesus name.

ACKNOWLEDGEMENT

My deepest gratitude goes to the HOLY SPIRIT for the divine unction to write this book.

My indepth gratitude goes to my beloved family; for loaning me to the world to fulfill the work of Ministry even as they shower me with their love, support and understanding. I do not take it for granted.

My sincere gratitude goes to the Editorial Team for the many hours of diligent labor to make this book a reality.

My special "thank you" goes to all the Staff and members of Nonnie Roberson Ministries, New Wine Outpouring Ministries, Sisterhood-Africa; to all my friends, and well-wishers who uphold me in prayer and contributed in one way or the other to the materialization of this book. I can't list you all... my heartfelt prayer is for God himself to reward you all immensely.

Finally, a very big "thank you" to everyone who directly or indirectly, helped to spread word about this book; may your reward not be few, and may the truth this book brings launch you to unprecedented fruitfulness in Jesus name.

Welcome to your world of fruitfulness!

PREFACE

Four years, she sat waiting. During an era where the worth of a woman was determined by one, getting married early, and two, bearing an heir or two. She had gotten married but was waiting patiently for the fruit of the womb. Not that she wasn't fertile; she conceived and miscarried severally… After series of miscarriages, one finally stayed through the period of pregnancy but alas, lived for only 8 months after birth. How devastated she felt! She desperately desired a living fruit of the womb.

That was my mother.

I was born from that womb. That womb that could not manage to bear a child that lived, gave birth to me after several years of seeking for the fruit of the womb. This time, she wanted my name to represent her pleas to God - "Nonyelum" which means "Stay with me, don't leave me". And then the flood gates were opened and I like to say that I ushered in four more children to my joyous parents without any more drama or delay.

Over the years, there has been strong evidence attesting to the UNUSUAL GRACE I carry for FRUITFULNESS; an unusual anointing that crushes the yoke of BARRENNESS.

It is a grace that I can't explain even to myself. People run to the altar when I make an altar call for the "Fruit of the Womb" to receive their blessing while others literally run out of the building as they have seen the miraculous results that have happened to those who come to the altar on behalf of their loved ones. Several women, including menopause grandmothers, have taken in just by coming out to stand in the gap for their loved ones believing God for the fruit of the womb.

In the first "FRUIT OF THE WOMB" program God led me to hold for women desiring the fruit of the womb, we recorded a 100% FRUITFULNESS within 3 months! Every woman who attended that program took in including those who came to stand in for their friends or relatives. From young women who were newly-weds, to the aged women of over 57 years of age.

This unusual grace that the Lord has given me often manifests itself in multiple births especially twins. And like the Bible says, charity begins at home, so I have a set of twins. My younger brother and my younger sister each have a set of twins too, by my prophetic declaration.

The Lord, by His grace has called me into a special ministry with a unique unction and grace in the area of fruitfulness which among other things, manifests in the fruit of the womb. By the special grace of God, and with all humility, I have seen multitudes of women with critical and hopeless cases receive amazing miracles in this area after a brief spiritual encounter. The testimonies of God's goodness to the women I have ministered to in the area of child-bearing are mind-blowing. Hence, anointing for breaking the yokes of bareness have become my trademark. This is my deal with Jehovah, the God of possibilities.

Now, not only do I have the special dispensation and grace for fruitful wombs, this dispensation also crosses over to all aspects of our lives and has prompted many to state, "No one hangs around Nonnie Roberson for 6 months without an evidence of fruitfulness in every area of their lives" This is to the glory of God and without doubt, I feel a great burden for all who seek for fruitfulness from our Father and he has given me this unique anointing that breaks the pangs of bareness off His people's neck.

"And I sought for a man among them that should make up the hedge, and stand in the gap before me for the land" - Ezekiel 22:30.

I feel the weight of God's daughters panting for children. I feel every tear, shame, and ridicule. I feel the weight of Daughters of Zion, sisters in Sisterhood-Africa, in despair… I feel the weight as God puts it on me like a second skin. As I cry out in agony, "God the weight is too much." He says to me "Daughter ask me for the capacity to carry it."

This weight compels me to intercede. It forces me to my knees and as I travail and groan on the floor, God visits his children and blesses them with their own children and perfects all that concerns them. Psalm 113:9 "He gives the barren woman a home, making her the joyous mother of children. Praise the Lord!"

God said in Mark 9:23, "To them that believe all things are possible" and He has instructed me to write a book to extend his mercy to the multitude. That book is "NONE SHALL BE BARREN" which is a complete armor for breaking and shattering every yoke of barrenness. The Lord has taught me that no case is hopeless as far as child-bearing is concerned and he has shown me that repeatedly.

He told me that the same Grace that rests on my life rests on this book by contact. He assured me that jaw dropping testimonies will abound.

Procreation is God's will for you. Don't let the devil cheat you of your right. Don't shed a tear any more. Rejoice, be glad, for I hear the cries of babies in your home, and remember "The Lord is your shepherd, you shall not want".

God's grace and mercy be with you.

Prophetess Nonnie Roberson

Founder, Nonnie Roberson Ministries

SECTION A
BARRENNESS IS NOT OF GOD

CHAPTER ONE

THE FRUIT OF THE WOMB IS A REWARD

"Lo, children are an heritage of the Lord:
And the fruit of the womb is his reward" (Ps. 127:3).

You have the right to birth good, healthy and beautiful children in the sexes of your choice. This is true because, children are a blessing from God. And the blessing of the Lord makes rich and does not add sorrow. Regardless of what the doctors have said concerning your case, what God says is what matters in the now. He has put His Word in my mouth, and I will declare it as I am commanded. God says His reward to you for being a wife and a husband is children. "The fruit of the womb is His reward" not His punishment. When He commanded that we should "multiply and replenish the earth" (Gen. 1:28), He meant every word of it. You were not excluded from those who were given seeds in the loins and eggs in the ovary. You are part and parcel of those who must multiply in the earth.

You are part and parcel of those who must multiply in the earth.

The earth is big enough to accommodate your own children just like it has accommodated the children of hundreds of millions of other mothers and fathers. He is not unjust to withhold any good thing from His children. God is not a respecter of persons (Acts 10:34). What He does for one person, He will do for another! Just as He did for Adam and Eve, He has continued to do till today. So your case cannot be an exception.

Infertility, no matter the coloration, is not of God. The Spirit of God ministered to me to rebuke those who now believe that it is God's will for them not to bear children. That is a lie from the devil to keep you deprived. If your heart's desire has been to experience the joy of childbirth, but you have not been able to do so thus far, you may feel that God does not want you to have children. You may feel that something is wrong with you and you don't deserve children. This simply is not the truth! The truth is that God has promised to give you the desires of your heart and He would not withhold any good thing from you (Ps. 37:4; 84:11; 145:16, 19). So you must cast that negative thought out of your mind. The fact that you have experienced delay does not mean it is God's will for you.

Procreation is God's will for you, not unfruitfulness. It is time to believe what God says concerning you. The reward of the fruit of the womb is your inheritance in God; you cannot let the devil steal it from you in any guise, whether through unbelief or the fear of your past mistakes. God is able to start you up on a clean slate. The fact that you have reproductive organs is an indication that you were meant to reproduce. You must resolve not to answer the name that God did not call you. He called you a fruitful vine (Ps.128:3).

You cannot afford to accept barrenness. Hannah did not accept it, so you must not accept it either.

> ***The fact that you have reproductive organs is an indication that you were meant to reproduce.***

There are abundant examples in the Bible of couples who were barren, but sought God for a change of status, and then later conceived and birthed incredible and influential children. In fact, there is no single case in the Bible where someone struggled with infertility and sought God and did not eventually conceive and birth a child! So, you are the next in the line in Jesus name.

Open the door of your heart to the possibility of having your own lovely children surrounding your table. See your sons and daughters and grand-children doting all over you. Imagine yourself giving your first child suck as a happy mother. Close your heart to unbelief and fear which comes by negative reports. You cannot afford to become lethargic no matter what has been said about your case. This is not the time for mental tiredness and despair. This is the time for aggressive faith.

God sent me to those who have cried enough, but who still have 'little' faith in God's ability and willingness to respond positively to their cases. If you are such a one, then you are the candidate I am sent to this hour. Your word for the hour is that God has heard your cries, and joy has entered into your house today. Sarah was made to laugh even when it was medically and biological impossible to conceive; your case is next on the line. By the time God is done with you, those who laughed at you will come and laugh with you. You will become a testimony of God's goodness and mercy. God will turn your pain to gain this year.

> *By the time God is done with you, those who laughed at you will come and laugh with you.*

You probably wonder if there will ever be a cry of a baby in your house, if you will ever have children to call you daddy and mummy. God said you should wonder no more; there is a performance of the very miracles you seek in Jesus name.

PRAYER EXERCISE

SCRIPTURE REFERENCE: (Ps. 127:3) "Lo, children are an heritage of the Lord: And the fruit of the womb is his reward".

PRAYER POINTS:

1. Father in the name of Jesus, I believe your word that you are my reward; thank you Father God for the reward of babies in my life in Jesus name.

2. Father God, I stand on the authority of your word, I rebuke the spirit of barrenness and I cast it out right now out of my life and the life of my spouse in Jesus name.

3. I receive the fruit of the womb right now (lay your hand on your womb as a wife, and hold your waist as a man). I command my seed to reproduce. I command my egg to fertilize now in Jesus name.

4. I command my children to come to me now, both boys and girls in Jesus name.

5. I rebuke you the spirit of miscarriage; I stand on the authority of Exodus 23:26 which says "There shall be no one miscarrying or barren in your land; I will fulfill the number of your days". I cast you spirit of miscarriage out of my life right now. Your yoke over my life is completely terminated in Jesus name – Amen!

SPIRITUAL DIRECTION: Let the couple take communion after these prayers at night before retiring to bed (1st day).

TESTIMONY: 10 years of Barrenness destroyed

I was barren for 10 years and in that ten years, I had gone through very agonizing moments, seen many doctors and even had failed IVF many times. When I heard of Prophetess Nonnie, I quickly decided that I will not go to the Prophetess especially since I had heard of many false prophets with false prophecies. So I just attended all the services. Then in one of those services, Prophetess Nonnie called me out and placed her hand on my stomach and said "I hear the heartbeat of a child", prayed for me and asked me to go back to my seat. Within a short time, I started experiencing the signs of pregnancy and so I decided to go for a check-up.

The first time I went for a scan, I was told that it cannot be pregnancy because there was no sac. The doctors mocked me, said there was no sac that I wouldn't be pregnant. I told God that I believe him, that the prophet said she heard the heartbeat of a child, sac or no sac I believed God. For three months there was still no sac as the Doctors said. Four months later, from no sac I was told it was a very large fibroid that must be taken out immediately, but I did not relent. I said, since I did not tell the Pastor anything and she said that there is a heartbeat of a child, then there must be a baby. I believed.

Prophetess Nonnie called me to come for prayers for those believing God for the fruit of the womb and pregnant women, but because I did not know where I belonged, I just told her I was busy. I believed that if the Pastor said that there is a heartbeat, then there must be a baby in my womb, though there was nothing to show me so. Then on the 7th month, the baby was picked on the scan!!!

What I was carrying all along was a baby and not fibroid and today, I am carrying this miracle baby in my hands. PRAISE THE LORD!!!

CHAPTER TWO

YOU ARE LIKE A FRUITFUL GRAPEVINE

"Your wife will be like a fruitful grapevine, flourishing within your home. Your children will be like vigorous young olive trees as they sit around your table" (Ps. 128:3)

The fact that God says you are a fruitful grapevine is exactly who you are. You are nothing short of what God calls you, medical reports notwithstanding. The report of the Lord supersedes all other reports, including doctors' diagnosis.

The olive tree and the grapevine are two of the most valuable gifts of nature in ancient Palestine. They are esteemed as the most valuable sources of revenue throughout most of Old Testament history e.g. 1 Sam. 8:14; 2 Kings 5:26. Its produce can be eaten fresh, dried for raisins, pressed for wine, or made into vinegar. Even the grape leafs are also used in recipes. So by comparing the fruitfulness of the woman to that of the grapevine, the Bible meant us to know that there is no place for unfruitfulness in the woman.

God created the woman so uniquely with the ability to carry life. No wonder Adam called his wife "the mother of all the living" (Gen. 3:20). God made the woman a life-giver. You cannot afford to settle for anything less. It is time to place a demand on your body and command it to fulfill purpose. I know you have prayed, fasted and even sown some financial seeds for the miracle of children; you have done well. However, God sent me to tell you not to give up hope. You are closer to your miracle than when you first started out on the journey of faith. What is expected of you is to press further. Continuity in faith is what causes undeniable breakthrough in life.

> **You cannot afford to settle for anything less. It is time to place a demand on your body and command it to fulfill purpose.**

Since we have agreed that it is God's will for you to be fruitful in your body, it is time to respond to the mountain of infertility with aggressive faith and the Spoken Word. Aggressive obstacles call for aggressive action. And aggressive faith mixed with the Word is the most potent force at your disposal. Keep calling those things that be not as though they are. Saturate yourself in the Word until faith springs forth and you believe the word of God more than you believe your natural circumstances, your doctors' diagnosis, cultural tales and predictions. All those reports in the natural may look real and convincing, but truth exists beyond what you can see, taste, hear, smell, or touch. It is time to stand on the confession of faith until your expectation is realized.

You may be questioning why you are experiencing delay or difficulties in the area of conception and delivery? The Lord said to me that it is because the seed in your loin is a special seed. You carry a seed of greatness and influence, which is why the devil is after your case. If you doubt me, take a look at the Scripture. Every child that was birthed after prolonged period of waiting all turned out to be special kids - from Isaac to Jacob and Esau, to Samuel and Samson, to John the Baptist, and our Lord and Savior Jesus Christ. They all had peculiar and unique assignment. That is what your case represents – a special assignment. And God sent me to tell you it is about time. But you have to behave like Mary. She said "let it be done to me according to your word" (Luke 1:38). It is time to bow your knees to Him in submission and lift your hands in adoration, and declare these words over your life. Don't just say the words; mean it as you say it. And then say it until you mean it. And there shall be a performance of the very thing spoken concerning you of the Lord.

> **You carry a seed of greatness and influence, which is why the devil is after your case.**

Stop complaining about your age. Faith is not limited by age or culture. Faith transcends both. "By faith Sarah herself also received strength to conceive seed, and she bore a child when she was past the age, because she judged Him faithful who had promised" (Heb. 11:11).

Faith is only limited by doubt and unbelief. It is not how old you are, but how well you can hold onto God that matters. God wants you to take off your eyes from the troubles and disappointments of yesterday and focus on the possibilities of today. That is what Hannah did. She went to Shiloh with a different perspective. She was not ready to leave with the same shame. She wanted a definite change to happen and it did. She was tired of telling the same story, shedding the same tears and hearing the same words from her husband Elkanah year in year out. She approached the matter with aggressive faith, and she was rewarded (Read 1 Samuel 1:9-19, 27).

You have just one thing between you and your fruitfulness, and that is your attitude. How you approach this issue is how it will respond to you. Grace is available now for your deliverance. As a child of God, your case is different. That is because of what Jesus did for us on the Cross; all believers are blessed with the blessings of faithful Abraham. Are you married to a person of the opposite sex? Are you a born-again believer? If yes, then the blessing of fruitfulness of the womb is already available to you. All you have to do is apply faith (confidence) in God's willingness and ability to make you fruitful and most assuredly, fruitfulness of the womb will be realized and appropriated to you. "Therefore do not cast away your confidence, which has great reward. For you have need of endurance, so that after you have done the will of God, you may receive the promise" (Heb. 10:35-36).

> *You have just one thing between you and your fruitfulness, and that is your attitude.*

Faith is a fight. Keep your confidence in God's Word and "Fight the good fight of faith." Fight for your fruitfulness. It is a worthy fight to engage in. So don't get tired of expecting your children. Don't get discouraged and give up, for we will reap a harvest of blessing at the appropriate time" (Gal. 6:9). And your appropriate time is now which is why you have this book in your hand.

The fact that God has said that "your children will be like vigorous young olive trees as they sit around your table" should ginger your expectation. Maybe you almost gave up hope after waiting for 10, 12, 15, or 20 years for the blessing of children. I have come with goodnews for you, it is time. Your morning has come and your night is over in Jesus name.

PRAYER EXERCISE

SCRIPTURE REFERENCE: (Ps. 128:3) "Your wife will be like a fruitful grapevine, flourishing within your home. Your children will be like vigorous young olive trees as they sit around your table".

PRAYER POINTS:

1. Father God, thank you for making me (my wife) like a fruitful grapevine, flourishing within my home. I am who you say I am in Jesus name.

2. Lord I decree that my own children from my womb (for the wife) and my loin (for the husband) will be like vigorous young olive trees as they sit around my table in Jesus name.

3. My Father God, I stand on the authority of your word and declare that this month is our month of visitation with the fruit of the womb in Jesus name.

4. In Jesus name, I cast out every power from the pit of hell, trying to weaken our fertility by fighting to weaken my wife's eggs and my husband's sperm.

5. Thank you Father God for answers to our prayers in Jesus name.

SPIRITUAL DIRECTION: The couple should take the communion for the second night after these prayers before retiring to bed (2nd day).

TESTIMONY: 12 years of Barrenness destroyed

I was married for 12 years with no child but on one faithful service, Prophetess Nonnie called me out and prayed for me and the next month, I was sick and when I went to the hospital, I was told that I was pregnant. I laughed at them and asked "if it is that easy?" because I have had series of tests that failed. To God be the glory, I am holding my child today.

CHAPTER THREE

DON'T ABANDON YOUR POSITIVE CONFESSION

"You shall be blessed above all peoples; there shall not be a male or female barren among you or among your livestock" (Deut. 7:14).

Your confession is your ticket to possibilities or impossibilities. It matters what you confess. If your confession is rooted on the promises of God, you shall also experience a performance of what God says. In the same vein, if your confession is at variance with what God has said to you, you are already sabotaging the grace that causes positive change to happen. So confess what you want to see happen to you.

You are what you say continuously. You cannot confess negative and see positive happen. In the same vein, you cannot maintain a positive declaration and experience negative occurrences. The happenings in your life are connected to the confessions of your mouth and the believing of your heart. Jesus said "out of the abundance of the heart the mouth speaketh" (Luke 6:46). Life is sowing and reaping. So be positive minded, not negative minded. No matter your experience, keep saying what the word of God says concerning your case. Don't abandon your positive confessions for negative ones because of delayed expectation. Don't close your mind to what God says because of disappointments. Don't lose hope of your miracle because of negative medical diagnosis. The grace of God is powerful enough to annul negative and scary medical reports. Your case is not irredeemable. There is still hope for conception for you as long as there is breath in you.

Don't abandon your positive confessions for negative ones because of delayed expectation.

Stop expecting to see your monthly period (for those trusting God for the fruit of the womb) after you are done reading this book and praying the prayers in it. It does not matter if you are seeing blood, keep speaking your fruitfulness. I have seen cases where I ministered to some women and they kept bleeding until few months to delivery. In the end they had their healthy children despite the issue of blood. So take your eyes away from the blood and see the blood of Christ sustaining your baby in the womb. The blood of Christ is the life-giving spirit that you carry as a believer. What you have is what you give. Since the blood of Christ flows through you, that is what the seed planted in your womb by your husband needs to grow.

God said to Jeremiah, before your mother conceived you in the womb I knew you, and ordained you a prophet to the nations (Jer. 1:5). That means that before the seed leaves your husband's loin and travels to meet your egg in the womb, God has already marked the child that is to be born. So stop crying because of blood. Rather, speak what God says over your life. You are not alone; God is with you in the situation. He knows you by name even before your mother conceived you, and had already chosen you for fruitfulness. That is why you were born with the organs of reproduction intact. That is what you have to see and confess consistently over your life.

What we say matters. What we refuse to say also matters. Some people are not guilty of what they confessed, but what they fail to confess. It is not enough to not be negative. You also must not keep silent in the face of satanic aggression. It is said that a closed mouth is a closed destiny. You must learn to say the right words over your life at the right time. Be proactive with your confession and not reactionary.

The Bible says in Colossians 4:6 "Let your speech be always with grace, seasoned with salt, that ye may know how ye ought to answer every man" (Col. 4:6). You must know how to rein in your thoughts and feelings before you can effectively answer the devil and those who may try to knock you down and run you over with their bad talk. You may not stop people from making you a talking point, but you can definitely stop their bad talk from defining your attitude, confessions and confidence level. Care more about what God thinks about you than the opinion of people. The world is heavily opinionated. Whatever you do or fail to do, will almost always attract people's opinion. Therefore, close your ears to them and open it to the Holy Spirit. If you go about listening to everything people say about you, your ears will get too heavy to hear what the Holy Spirit is saying to you. What the Holy Spirit says is what really matters to your life.

An interesting example of consistent positive declaration is seen in 2 kings 4:8-37. That is the account of the Shunamite woman. She had every reason to yell "why me Lord" after her miracle son whom God had given her had died all of a sudden. However she did not. When her husband asked her why she was travelling to go see the Prophet, she could have broken down in tears for her loss, instead she responded with "it is well". When the Prophet sent his servant to ask her whether all was well with her and her family, she could have cursed him out in her pain, but she did not do any of that. She did not speak negativity to people who could not help her; instead she confessed "It is well". We also learn from this Shunamite woman that she only said what she wanted to see happen, she never once confessed that her son was dead, because she knew that the same God who gave her the son is able to raise him from the dead. And her faith was rewarded.

> *If you go about listening to everything people say about you, your ears will get too heavy to hear what the Holy Spirit is saying to you.*

Positive declaration does not mean denying the obvious; it means echoing what God says despite the obvious. What is obvious is a mere fact; what God says is the ultimate truth. God says there shall not be male or female barren in the land. This is not just a prophecy for the Jews any longer. It is a word for the hour to the child of God who by virtue of redemption has become a spiritual Israelite. I don't care who has concluded on you other than God, it is your season of celebration. As Sarah was celebrated for the birth of Isaac, you shall be celebrated for the birth of your own Isaac. It shall be said of you "He makes the barren woman to keep house, and to be a joyful mother of children. Praise ye the LORD" (Ps. 113:9).

> *God says there shall not be male or female barren in the land.*

I prophesy over your life, from this hour your story has changed. The yoke of barrenness is broken in Jesus name.

PRAYER EXERCISE

SCRIPTURE REFERENCE: (Deut. 7:14) "You shall be blessed above all peoples; there shall not be a male or female barren among you or among your livestock".

PRAYER POINTS:

1. O Lord my God, I thank you for the promise that "there shall not be a male or female barren among you or among your livestock". I thank you because I am marked for fruitfulness.

2. Father God, I command my womb to come alive. I decree that I am marked for signs and wonders of conception and I shall deliver according to the time of life in Jesus name.

3. I declare that I am blessed and not cursed. I am a celebration not an object of caricature in Jesus name

4. Every power fighting against my childbirth, your time is up, be cast into the bottomless pit by the power of the Holy Spirit. Your assignment over my life is over. I am free in Jesus name.

5. I declare, I am a joyful mother of children. My husband is a joyful father of children, according to the word of the Lord in Jesus name.

6. I decree that those who mocked me because of my childlessness will come and rejoice with me in the next nine months in Jesus name.

7. Thank you Father God for answers to prayers in Jesus name.

SPIRITUAL DIRECTION: The couple should take the Holy Communion after the prayers tonight before retiring to bed (3rd day).

TESTIMONY: I heard what God was doing through Prophetess Nonnie...

I heard what God was doing through Prophetess Nonnie and because I had been barren for 10 years and lived in Port Harcourt, I decided to go all the way to Abuja. I sought for and found Prophetess Nonnie. I was waiting to meet an old woman, but I met this beautiful yuppie, tastefully dressed lady, who is soft spoken with American accent. She sent me to the church's prayer team who started praying for me as I cried, upset that she didn't want to come and see me. While they were praying, she came in and told me that she was inquiring from God what my issue was, and God told her to tell me that I was pregnant. I told her that I have never been pregnant in my life, she said God said I should go that I was pregnant and I should come back in three days with a bottle of anointing oil and I should go get a pregnancy test done. To

God be the glory, yes I am pregnant, when and how it happened I don't know. To God be all the glory.

CHAPTER FOUR

KNOW YOUR HEALTH STATUS

"I am the Lord who heals you" (Ex. 15:26).

God is interested in your total wellbeing. There is a close relationship between your physical wellbeing and your spiritual wellbeing, as well as your mental wellbeing. The Apostle John states it succinctly, "Beloved, I pray that you may prosper in all things and be in health, just as your soul prospers" (3 John 2). Apostle John affirms the fact that God is interested in your health. However, God expects you to take matters of your health seriously too. Our spirit, soul and body are gifts from God, and He expects us to take good care of them. That is why it is important to know your health status as you trust God for the miracle of children. Health status here is not limited to medical health alone. Sometimes the problems are spiritual. So if your spiritual health is under demonic attacks, you need to handle it spiritually as well. In any case, God is above all and has promised to handle all for the hurting.

Knowing your health status is not to scare you but to help you to be better guided in your prayers and expectation. If your medical report is not favorable, it is good to consult medical experts so to at least get their opinion. In the same vein, if your medical is okay and you still struggle to conceive, it is a sign that you have to do more spiritual work on your case. Whatever is your situation, be aware of what is happening to and in you. That way you can be in charge and not be in the dark. Awareness is power. Ignorance is a weakness.

> ***Knowing your health status is not to scare you but to help you to be better guided in your prayers and expectation.***

Once you are aware of what is happening to and in you, the next thing is to know how to act in faith and appropriate the mind of God over your situation. The Scripture reveals to us the mind of God in several passages. Here are a few of them: "I will take away sickness from among you" (Ex. 23:25-26). Whether your sickness is spiritual, psychological, medical or even financial, God has promised to take it away from you. David declares: "He forgives all my sins and heals ALL my Diseases" (Ps. 103:3). Again He says in Jer. 30:17, "For I will restore health unto thee, and I will heal thee of thy wounds, saith the LORD; because they called thee an Outcast, saying, this is Zion, whom no man seeketh after." God says because people badmouth you for your predicaments, I will give you back your health again and heal your wounds." This means that it really does not matter how complicated the situations that affect your childbirth are, God can and will fix it. Moses also declares: "The Lord will remove from you all sickness. . ." (Deut. 7;15), and cause you to be fruitful in the land. Moses knew God well enough to know the mind of God concerning His children. He said "God will remove ALL sickness from you". These are amazing promises of God to His children who may be afflicted by any form of diseases. So even if your efforts are sabotaged by infirmity, you can tap into God's provision for your health. His promises to you are yea and amen. He is dependable and trustworthy.

Another reason why it is important for you to know your health status is to enable you appraise the situation and avoid any known practices that could trigger and aggravate the situation. For instance, excessive smoking and alcohol are said to be harmful to the reproductive system. Therefore, if you are addicted to these or other substances that are detrimental to your health, you may want to cut down on the volume of intake or at best stop the habit completely. God wants to give you healthy children, and He also wants you to stay alive healthily to raise them.

Another benefit of knowing your health status is to enable you to appreciate the gift of life. A person may not appreciate divine health until he has at least once been on admission in the hospital. Life is sacred, and it is a gift of God. Your ability to appreciate God for your life can open doors for other wonderful blessings including that of conception. So be grateful for life. If you cannot thank God for your life, how then would you thank Him when He adds another life to you? Thankfulness is a sign of responsibility, but ungratefulness is a sign of irresponsibility. God takes note of how you handle your body before He gives you that special seed to bring to the world. Your health is your wealth, treat your body well. Eat right and exercise moderately. Watch against gluttony, obesity, and depression because they trigger emotional imbalance. Keep fit both physically and spiritually, and remain positive minded with confidence in God and all will be well.

> *Your health is your wealth, treat your body well.*

My prayer for you is that you will be healed of every infirmity hampering your conception in Jesus name.

PRAYER EXERCISE

SCRIPTURE REFERENCE: "I am the Lord who heals you" (Ex. 15:26).

PRAYER POINTS:

1. Lord Jesus, I thank you for being my healer and deliverer, receive praise.
2. Father God, thank you for the gift of life; because you live, I shall face tomorrow in Jesus name.
3. Father God, I receive deliverance from every infirmity working against my conception today in Jesus name.

4. O Lord my God, anywhere I may have contributed to my childlessness, I plead your mercy by the blood of Jesus over my life today in Jesus name.

5. O Lord my God, I receive my testimony today in Jesus name.

SPIRITUAL DIRECTION: The couple should take the Communion after the prayers before retiring to bed (4th day).

TESTIMONY: 25 years of Barrenness destroyed

Mine is the case of Sarah. I am over 50 years old, married for 25 years with no issues. I live in Lagos. I have done so many unsuccessful IVF's and fertility treatment which failed. I have gone to all parts of the world looking for the fruit of the womb. I had retired to fate and actually given up when I heard what God was doing through the woman of God, I flew from Lagos to see her and when I met her I was disappointed. She had well-manicured nails with red polish, her face perfectly made up, she was pretty though, wore jeans and a fez cap. I thought to myself, I should be leading this one to the Lord and not her leading me, but when it was time for prayers, fire came out of her mouth. I was struck down under the anointing. She told me to go for IVF again and referred me to a doctor; she said 'God said He'll do it'. I told her I have had many failed IVF's, but reluctantly I agreed to trust God again. She prayerfully monitored and followed me through every phase. To God be the glory I am carrying a bouncing baby boy.

CHAPTER FIVE

DON'T GIVE UP ON YOUR SPOUSE

"Even when there was no reason for hope, Abraham kept hoping--believing that he would become the father of many nations. For God had said to him, "That's how many descendants you will have!" (Rom. 4:18).

The first mistake couples who are searching for the miracle of fruit of the womb make is to begin to play the blame game. I mean a situation where the husband begins to blame the wife and her people as the cause of his predicament, and the wife also blames the husband for the cause of her childlessness. The blame game is Satan's trick to distract your focus and fortify the problem. Rather than blame each other, as believers, you have to be there for one another despite medical report.

I have seen cases where the husband accuses the wife and the wife accuses the husband. I have also seen where they blame childlessness on infections. While not undermining or ruling out the possibility of these factors to cause damages, I dare say they are mere symptoms. The devil remains the number one enemy against your joy of fruitfulness. Have you ever wondered how the mad woman conceives and gives birth to a child without attending anti-natal or living in a hygienic environment and eating hygienic food? Whatever becomes of such children is only God that can tell. However, the battle is not against your spouse my dear: "For we wrestle not against flesh and blood, but against principalities, against powers, against the rulers of the darkness of this world, against spiritual wickedness in high places" (Eph. 6:12). So take the battle to where it belongs —the camp of the devil.

> *The devil remains the number one enemy against your joy of fruitfulness.*

There is no infection that cannot bow to the force of prayers if it surmounts medications. So, rather than get embittered with one another, love and care more for one another. Make the devil go mad with your love for one another. The blame game has never helped any family, rather, it destroys marriages. Once the two of you have decided to enter the holy union, you have become "one flesh". As one flesh, you cannot be seen fighting against your body. So take away the bitterness and focus on the main issue. You may not be able to undo your past life, but you can recreate the future of your dream by the power of the Holy Spirit and total submission to the Lord.

God is interested in your family today as much as He was interested in Abraham's family. The Bible says that Abraham "hoped against hope" (Rom. 4:18). He did not consider his body dead or the deadness of Sarah's womb. Whether Sarah was already beyond menopause was not a consideration. He did not harass and blame Sarah for the cause of his childlessness even when he had reasons to do so. After all he had already proven his virility by the birth of Ishmael. So Abraham loved Sarah and honored her despite the challenge of childlessness. So don't go hating on and depriving your partner, but seek God's mercy in all things.

> **God is interested in your family today as much as He was interested in Abraham's family.**

The fear of menopause has driven a lot of women insane already. Don't be caught in the web. Only God is to be feared. Menopause is an experience not a death sentence. Children are gifts from the Lord. And menopause does not limit God's ability. Women are giving birth freely at old age these days. This is an ageless season. So don't let the devil pollute your hearts with blame game. Neither your wife nor your husband is the real problem. The devil is! Our Lord Jesus calls him the thief, who comes to steal, and kill, and destroy (Jn.10:10). And because the devil hates a happy union, he wants to steal it from you – don't let him.

The account of the childlessness of Elizabeth and her husband Zechariah readily comes to mind. The Bible says in Luke 1:7b that both of them were very old. That does not sound encouraging at all. They must have been well over sixty years. They were well advanced in years. That depicts a situation where it seems like time is running out on you – you seem to be running late. It may be that you have entered your dark hour. Everyone has written you off by reason of your childlessness. Maybe the pressure from family is mounting to an unbearable stage and you are considering a way out. God has sent me to you with a simple message of this book, and that is that your time of deliverance has come. However, I need to remind you here that you have to keep hope alive. You have to keep the peace with your spouse, and most importantly, your love for one another must overshadow the hate of the devil against your union.

Life is not necessarily about duration but donation. It does not matter who has gone ahead of you, there is always room for overtaking in life. Elkanah's second wife, Peninnah had 10 sons for him while Hannah had none. In the end, it was Hannah's first son, Samuel that became the most influential man in Israel at the time. Samuel remains one of the most feared and influential prophets that ever led Israel. He was the moral compass of the nation of Israel; whereas there was not even one mention of the names or the exploits of the sons of Peninnah in the Bible. So what matters is what you are doing now about your case. This book has come with a clear and simple message of what to do.

> **Life is not necessarily about duration but donation. It does not matter who has gone ahead of you, there is always room for overtaking in life.**

Zechariah did not make his wife a scapegoat. He did not blame the situation on his wife. He also did not blame it on God. He could have exonerated himself from the situation by divorcing Elizabeth and perhaps marry a younger woman and make children from her since barrenness was a commonly acceptable ground for divorce in their society. That was the route many other men would have taken, but not Zechariah. Instead he prayed. He trusted God who can do exceeding abundantly above all that we may ask or imagined, according to the power that works in us (Eph. 3:20). I don't know what cases you think cannot be reopened. I am sent to announce to you that that case is not hopeless. God is cooking something special for your family and in 9 months' time, it will drop in Jesus name.

Another mistake couples who are challenged in this area make, is that they allow life's ugly situation to reconfigure them from nice people to highly temperamental people. Some even change from being faithful believers to unfaithful, unholy ones, just to prove that they are mad at God. I have seen situations where someone, because of delay in childbearing turns from a God-fearing Christian to a backslider, from a fervent believer to a nominal Christian, and from serving faithfully in the house of God to withdrawing and criticizing everything and everyone. You don't have to get 'mad' at God. That is not the way to go my dear. Rather than run from God, hold tighter onto Him in your time of despair: "For God is not unrighteous to forget your work and labour of love, which ye have shewed toward his name, in that ye have ministered to the saints, and do minister" (Heb. 6:10).

Imagine if Zechariah had become angry at God and quit the ministry. Imagine if Elizabeth had committed suicide because of her shame. But no, they kept serving. Zechariah may have read the account of Abraham's childlessness and God's intervention over and over again. Elizabeth may have also read the story of Rebekah and Hannah over and over. There was the realization that it is not about he that willeth or runneth, but God who showeth mercy.

> ***God is cooking something special for your family and in 9 months' time, it will drop in Jesus name.***

Here is your Rhema (revealed word from God for the hour): "And we desire that every one of you do show the same diligence to the full assurance of hope unto the end: That ye be not slothful, but followers of them who through faith and patience inherit the promises" (Heb.

6:12). Because you have been faithfully and patiently waiting for God, receive your miracle in Jesus name.

PRAYER EXERCISE

SCRIPTURE REFERENCE: "Even when there was no reason for hope, Abraham kept hoping--believing that he would become the father of many nations. For God had said to him, "That's how many descendants you will have!" (Rom. 4:18)

PRAYER POINTS:

1. O Lord my God, I thank you for the promise of childbearing, I key into the blessings of Abraham in Jesus name.

2. Father God, I receive grace to hope against hope like Abraham and Sarah. I decree that my expectation shall not be cut short in Jesus name.

3. My Father God, I stand against every power fighting against the realization of my expectation, I cast those powers out to the abyss in Jesus name.

4. You spirit of childlessness, you have no place in my life and in the life of my spouse, I dismantle your stronghold in my life in Jesus name.

5. I decree, according to the word of God, that none shall be barren; I am a fruitful vine in Jesus name.

6. Thank you Father God for answers to prayers. I receive my miracle babies today in Jesus name. Amen!

SPIRITUAL DIRECTION: The couple should take the Communion after the prayers tonight before retiring to bed. (5th day)

TESTIMONY: Indeed, unusual grace for the fruit of the womb rests on Prophetess Nonnie

I can attest to the unusual grace Prophetess Nonnie carries when it comes to the fruit of the womb matters; it's amazing! I have heard and seen testimonies that made me reverence God and wonder how such a woman so unassuming can walk in such power. My husband and I decided to have three kids, we had finished giving birth. Prophetess Nonnie was on that faithful day praying for those believing God for the fruit of the womb and asked people to come and stand in the gap for anyone we knew in that category, our loved ones and so on. I came out to stand in the gap for my sister and that was it, I became pregnant!

Now when Prophetess Nonnie is praying for women believing God for the fruit of the womb, I run out of the building. I am not the only one this has happened to, even pregnant women are scared to stand in the gap for people, the anointing is so real and potent that a menopausal woman can get pregnant under the unusual grace this woman of God carries. The anointing is truly overflowing and I am a living proof.

CHAPTER SIX

PREPARE FOR YOUR MIRACLE BABY

"Now the LORD was gracious to Sarah as he had said, and the LORD did for Sarah what he had promised. Sarah became pregnant and bore a son to Abraham in his old age, at the very time God had promised him"
(Gen. 21:1-2).

The Lord asked me to tell you to prepare for that miracle child you are looking for: it shall no more tarry says the Spirit of the Lord. So my dear, it is time to prepare. You must prepare spiritually, mentally, physically and otherwise. The reason for the preparation is because you are about to birth a great destiny into this world. Just like in the case of Samson where his mother was told to prepare for his arrival into this world for a special assignment, I have been instructed to inform you to prepare for that baby you have been waiting for. Here are some ways you must prepare for the child:

> *I have been instructed to inform you to prepare for that baby you have been waiting for.*

a. Spiritual preparation: Spiritual preparation is the state of clearing out negative spiritual atmosphere for the child. A lot of people are suffering unnecessary spiritual attacks today because nobody cleared their family or ancestral darkness before they were born. Some are going through harrowing experiences because of the spiritual atmosphere of their family. So if you want your miracle children to fight fewer battles than what you fought to get to where you are today, pray ahead of them. King Solomon had no battles to fight throughout his reign because his father King David had fought all the battles. So Solomon's reign saw peace and great prosperity. You are expected to prophesy into the life and the destiny of that child great things that you want to see happen. This is the state where you call those things that be not as though they were. This is the moment to see that child (children) in the eyes of your spirit, and write down their names for them. While Abraham was still childless, God took him outside for an encounter with spiritual reality: "And the Lord brought Abram outside [his tent into the night] and said, "Look now toward the heavens and count the stars—if you are able to count them." Then He said to him, "So [numerous] shall your descendants be" (Gen. 15:5). Eventually God fulfilled His promise to Abraham; Sarah conceived and gave birth to a son according to Genesis 21. This is the time to speak into the destinies of the children you are trusting God for. And as you say it, there shall be a performance in Jesus name. Just when Abraham was despairing of not having an heir, God promised him descendant too numerous to imagine. That promise has continued to be a reality till date. Now it is your turn. If you can see it in the eye of your spirit, you will be more joyful from this moment than you have ever been.

> **This is the time to speak into the destinies of the children you are trusting God for.**

b. Mental preparation: This has to do with developing a positive mentality about yourself and about the child you are expecting. This is so important especially for the woman who has come of age. There are some diseases that are associated with late conception, which bothers women whenever they think about their age. So you got to be mentally strong for the child. Don't entertain fear because your case is different. Your emotion must be stable. Fight emotional instability vigorously because emotional instability can lead to hormonal imbalance which is capable of affecting conception. This is the time to be at your best. Your body needs you to be at your best so as to be able to accommodate that miracle baby; yours is a special child, which is why your experience is different. Abraham was told that as far as his eyes could see would be his for possession. "The LORD said to Abram after Lot had parted from him, "Look around from where you are, to the north and south, to the east and west" (Gen. 13:14).

c. Physical preparation: This is very crucial. You must be ready physically, and that includes financially. Don't fail to buy baby things whether you are medically certified pregnant or not. It is an act of faith to buy baby things while waiting. Get a convenient environment for your child. Neaten your house regularly. Make room for the baby. Let your faith drive you to positive action. It does not matter how foolish your enthusiasm may appear in the eyes of people; in God's eyes you are acting your faith. And your faith is what brings God into your affairs. Apostle James says that we must show our faith by our works (Jas. 2:18). We also went further to say that "Faith without works is dead" (Jas. 2:26). My prayer for you is that as you act on these words by faith, they will yield the expected results for you in Jesus name.

> *Make room for the baby. Let your faith drive you to positive action.*

PRAYER EXERCISE

SCRIPTURE REFERENCE: "Now the LORD was gracious to Sarah as he had said, and the LORD did for Sarah what he had promised. Sarah became pregnant and bore a son to Abraham in his old age, at the very time God had promised him." (Gen. 21:1-2).

PRAYER POINTS:

1. Thank you Father God for being a promise-keeping God; as you kept your promise to Abraham, you shall do same for me in Jesus name.

2. O Lord my God, I cast out the spirit of unbelief from my spirit; from today, I will believe you without hesitation in Jesus name.

3. My Father God, I decree that every strange spiritual personality responsible for my childlessness be judged now in Jesus name.

4. Father God, as Sarah bore Abraham a son and as Abraham's seed was strong enough to fertilize Sarah's egg so shall it be for us in Jesus name

5. Thank you Lord Jesus for answers to prayers, I receive my miracle child now in Jesus name.

SPIRITUAL DIRECTION: The couples who have prayed these prayers shall take the Communion tonight before retiring to bed (6th day).

TESTIMONY: 6 years of Barrenness destroyed

I have been married for 6 years, each time I get pregnant, I see a particular aunt of mine in the dream and when I wake, I'll lose the pregnancy. I told the woman of God after someone had invited me to meet her; she told me that there was a wedding gift I was given that was at the entrance. I couldn't remember the gift, the woman of God drew it out for me and I recollected, she told me to go and burn it that God said I'll be pregnant within 3 months, to God be the glory I am holding my miracle baby

SECTION B
FIGHT FOR YOUR FRUITFULNESS

CHAPTER SEVEN

BATTLE AGAINST ENEMIES OF YOUR FRUITFULNESS

"And from the days of John the Baptist until now the kingdom of heaven suffereth violence, and the violent take it by force" (Matt. 11:12).

Life is a battle ground. You must be warfare conscious and ready at all times to engage the enemies of your all-round fruitfulness. The battle of life is a real one. The devil is still the devil and his mission to hate on the believer has not changed. He is never going to be a nice devil any day neither will he ever stop trying to kill your joy and make your life miserable. He is always searching for a loophole to explore for his selfish aim. You have to be alert in the spirit in other to checkmate him effectively.

Fruitfulness is God's design for your life. He wants you to bear an abiding fruit and prosper even as your soul prospereth. He has provided everything needed for the good life for the believer so that we have no reason to fail. But then, it is our responsibility to appropriate that which God has provided for us. And since the devil is bent on seeing us deprived, we must be bent on casting him out of our lives on a daily basis.

The powers wanting to stop your testimonies are working, so you cannot afford to become complacent in life. So friends, don't mistake the uncomfortable direction your life is turning as the will of God for you, as it is not everything that is happening to you that has the approval of God. There are traces of the hand of the enemy in all bad things that come our way if we look through the lens of the spirit. The fact that God is aware of everything that comes our way does not necessarily mean it is His will for us to suffer. We still have the devil here trying to superimpose his will on us and that is why we have to be alert in the spirit to stop him. God already has given us what it takes to stop him, which is why it is pertinent for us to battle the enemies of our fruitfulness with every divine weapon in our arsenal.

Since the devil is bent on seeing us deprived, we must be bent on casting him out of our lives on a daily basis.

According to our text, the kingdom of God is forcefully advancing and only "violent" men take it by force. This means there is a war that rages behind the scene. It is a spiritual war. Life is not just ordinary. Only the ones who "press" forward can be victorious. Every kind of war is violent, and there is no exception to this issue of your fruitlessness. Unless you are "violent"- having holy zeal and determination, you will never win it. You have got to strive and press forward every inch in this spiritual battle. If you are hoping to be victorious doing nothing about it, you will prolong the affliction. You have to strive for your fruitfulness in whatever area you are being shortchanged. We strive and wrestle it out not physically with our fellow humans, but spiritually with the powers of darkness which can possess humans to carry out their nefarious activities. The Apostle Paul wrote: "For we wrestle not against flesh and blood, but against principalities, against powers, against the rulers of the darkness of this world, against spiritual wickedness in high places" (Eph. 6:12).

Uncover that enemy

Until you put your problems in perspective, you will lack the knowledge to handle them. And one of the ways you uncover or identify them is through their characteristics. Matthew 13:25 tells us, "But while men slept, his enemy came and sowed tares among the wheat, and went his way." Enemies will always come to undo, fight and hinder what you have done. These powers are the reason why your life lacks color today. They are the reason why you are still at that same level year after year. These powers are out to frustrate your life and deny you the possession of the good life which you deserve. Don't take it lightly that you still have not had a child many years after marriage. It is not God's will my dear. An enemy has caused it and that enemy has to be uprooted wherever it is hiding.

When an enemy sows tares in a marriage, terrible and mysterious things happen to couples. Multiple pregnancies without children are one of them. Multiple miscarriages are not just accidents or coincidences; they are orchestrated by demonic forces to destroy your marriage. Misfortunes are not just ordinary; they are spiritually designed by the devil to limit our possibilities. So this is not the time to be indolent and complacent in matters of your destiny. Why should a pregnant woman see a red cloth in her dream only to wake and have a miscarriage? That cannot be ordinary. It is the enemy sowing tares to corrupt her wheat (pregnancy). Why should a married man and woman be having regular sexual intercourse in the dream with strange people? That cannot be ordinary too; it should be a thing of concern to the victims. Some women put to birth in the dream but cannot conceive in the physical. That is one of the ways the devil uses witchcraft to corrupt the seeds and the eggs in the couple. Some babies that are born deformed are products of such unconventional intercourse. Marriage is supposed to be a blessing and not a curse. A situation where your life spirals on a downward slid after marriage is not of God. I have seen a situation where a couple did every necessary test and were both certified okay by more than three gynecologists before marriage, only for the story to change after wedding. The man who was certified virile suddenly had low sperm-count and the wife had multiple fibroids in her womb. Strange things happen because of strange powers fighting against the destinies of people. This is not a time to sleep. It is a dangerous time we live in.

> *Misfortunes are not just ordinary; they are spiritually designed by the devil to limit our possibilities.*

The farmer sowed wheat and he was looking forward to fruitfulness, but beside all the wheat he sowed, his enemy sowed tares. What was the work of the tares? Of course to choke the wheat and stop it from producing, thereby running the farmer bankrupt.

Many couples have sleepless nights constantly because of the reality of the troubles of life. Some get broke every month because of multiple medical bills due to all manners of fertility tests. Like the woman with the issue of blood in Mathew 5:21-43, you may have wasted your earnings in the hands of many physicians without headway. That should cause you to put your problem in proper perspective. In the parable of the wheat and the tares, the farmer was able to identify the fact that "an enemy has done this" (Matt. 13:28). You need to identify just where your battles (strongholds) are located. Once you begin to identify the battles, you need to wage war against them.

Use God's strategy to battle them

The Bible says that by strength (human effort) shall no man prevail (1 Sam. 2:9). Therefore, you need to deploy God's strategy in dealing with the enemies of your fruitfulness. In 2 Cor. 10:3-5, we are instructed on how to war against battles (strongholds), where Satan launches his attacks. For though we walk in the flesh, we do not war according to flesh; for the weapons of our warfare are not carnal but mighty in God for pulling down strongholds. Casting down arguments and every high thing that exalts itself against the knowledge of God, bringing down every thought into captivity to the obedience of Christ.

> *You have everything it takes to be fruitful in life; don't let the devil tell you otherwise.*

Take note of the following:

- The battle is not physical: this not a conventional battle; it is a spiritual battle and must be fought in the spiritual realm.

- Our weapons are able to pull down strongholds and high things because they are mighty through God. This is a call not to undermine or underestimate the potency of the weapons at your disposal as a believer. Proper evaluation of your placement in God is a veritable tool that can enhance your confidence level in the fight.

- The fight is against that which exalts itself against the knowledge of God (the Word) in your life. This means that anything discrediting your testimony must be fought against.

- Victory is achieved by bringing every thought into captivity of the obedience of Christ. There is no room for doubt and fear as we fight. We fight with the authority of our Lord and Savior Jesus Christ.

Satan knows that if you are able to remove these strongholds, you will be able to take hold of your fruitfulness, so he uses subterfuge to bound people. Until these powers are arrested and destroyed, you may never be able to achieve your dreams in life. Life calls for striving. It calls for battles. It calls for tenacity. It calls for courageous action. If you are not ready for the battles of life, you are not ready for the joy of fruitfulness.

In this book, I have set out on a journey to lead you to your fruitfulness. My intention has been to help you demystify the enemies of your fruitfulness, dismantle their strongholds over your life and enjoy all that God has in store for you.

You have no reason to remain unfruitful in your marriage. You have no reason to be the down trodden in your family. You have no reason to live in perpetual shame and agony. You have no reason to remain an average in life. You were meant for fruitfulness, you cannot settle for anything less. As long as a man is satisfied with where he is, next level is a fairy tale to him; however, the moment there is dissatisfaction with where you are, you are ready to step up to a new level.

> *If you are not ready for the battles of life, you are not ready for the joy of fruitfulness.*

Fruitfulness does not happen by wishes but by enforcement. Too many wishes fail because of a lack of enforcement. Unfruitfulness is a misrepresentation of your true nature in Christ; it is a deviation and a negation to your original configuration in destiny. A man is meant to be a father and a woman is created to be a mother. That is how you were wired by God. Nothing short of that is acceptable.

PRAYER EXERCISE

SCRIPTURAL REFERENCE: "God blessed them and said to them, "Be fruitful and increase in number; fill the earth and subdue it. Rule over the fish in the sea and the birds in the sky and over every living creature that moves on the ground." (Gen. 1:28)

PRAYER POINTS:

1. My Father God, I take a stand against every power fighting against my fruitfulness. I command them to catch fire now in the name of Jesus.

2. You powers from my mother's or father's linage fighting against my all-round fruitfulness, your time is up – be rooted out now and cast to the bottomless pit in Jesus name.

3. All witchcraft spirits monitoring my marital destiny, be blinded now by the power of the Holy Spirit in Jesus name.

4. Every altar speaking evil over my marriage, catch fire now in Jesus name.

5. You spirit that eats up children in the womb and cause miscarriages, I rebuke you over my life. Every access you have had to my womb is plucked now in Jesus name.

6. You spiritual husband and spiritual wife, I terminate your access to my life whether in the dream or in the physical. I decree enough is enough, no more access to you in Jesus name.

7. Every damage and affliction in my life as a result of the defilement by unauthorized and

unconventional intercourse is thereby annulled in Jesus name.

8. I am free indeed because the Son of God has set me free in Jesus name.

SPIRITUAL DIRECTION

The couple shall take the communion after praying these prayers before retiring to bed (7th day).

TESTIMONY: 4 years of Barrenness destroyed

The Lord laid it in my heart to sow a prophetic seed in the life of the woman of God. After I did, she called me back. I have been believing God for the fruit of the womb for 4 years, she placed her hand on my tummy, prayed and told me to get ready that I'll be pregnant soon. My husband has been out of the town, and was coming in that night. I was due for my monthly cycle and the woman of God did something crazy. She said, "ovulation come back, period I forbid you from coming out tonight", lo and behold I never saw my period again; I took in that night. My beautiful daughter is an evidence of God's faithfulness and goodness

CHAPTER EIGHT

BATTLE AGAINST CURSES AND ITS CONSEQUENCES

"Like a flitting sparrow, like a flying swallow, so a curse without cause shall not alight (Prov. 26:2).

Curses and their consequences are real, and a lot of nice people are groaning daily as a result of the consequences of a curse. A curse in this context is a demonic meddling in a person which causes a pattern of negative occurrences in the life of that individual. A curse can also come from God as we shall see shortly.

A curse is a destiny saboteur. Its agenda is to keep a person perpetually disadvantaged in life. A person's life, for example, may have a history of disappointment and tragedy. Marriages may be under constant strain. There may be recurrence of accidents and illnesses, bad-luck and hard-life. Desired goals may not materialize, and the lingering sense of failure and frustration may be evident. A person may even struggle continually against an unidentifiable situation which brings endless frustration or something blocking him or her, and no matter how hard the person tries, it feels like there is a wall stopping his or her progress.

> *A curse is a destiny saboteur. Its agenda is to keep a person perpetually disadvantaged in life.*

A curse is like hitting a brick wall. So the man and woman who want to make headway in life must battle against all kinds of curses. Once you notice a strange pattern of losses and struggles in your life, you must raise a strong spiritual battle because a curse may just be the cause. I once ministered to a woman who had had three miscarriages, and each of them happened in the same number of months — the fifth month. Under further scrutiny, I realized there was something about the fifth month in their family history. Her grand-father had died in the fifth month. Her father also died in the fifth month. The most painful is that she lost her younger brother under very suspicious circumstances in the fifth month. It was like the fifth month was a tragic one for her – a month of deaths. That is a terrible pattern. We had to embark on a serious spiritual exercise and rededication to Christ to break that curse before this woman could be free from the fear of death and have a baby. Sometimes a pattern runs in families even as far back as great-grandparents. I have seen a situation where a great-grandfather had one son and many daughters, the grandfather also had one son and many daughters, and the only son now has five daughters and one son. Again that is a pattern. But the goodnews is that a curse is not absolute; it can be stopped. Whatever curse or negative pattern operating in your life will be stopped today in Jesus name!

Truth is some infertility and financial setbacks are demonic-curse related. And until they are broken, a couple may end up childless and penniless. There are also few examples of God inflicted curses as seen in the Scripture. It happened to the women in the house of Abimelek when he took Sarah, Abraham's wife. The Bible says "for the LORD had kept all the women in Abimelek's household from conceiving because of Abraham's wife Sarah" (Gen. 20:18). It happened also to Hannah in 1 Sam. 1:4-20. The Bible says that her womb was shut by the Lord. The Bible in her case didn't tell us why her womb was shut by the Lord. We see how it happened also to Michal, the daughter of King Saul who was married to David. The account has it that she died childless because she despised King David in her heart because of how David danced and rejoiced over the Ark of the Lord. (Read 2 Sam. 6:16-23). There are many situations people go through which reinforces the operationality of a curse.

> ***Truth is some infertility and financial setbacks are demonic-curse related. And until they are broken, a couple may end up childless and penniless.***

According to our text; "A curse without a cause shall not alight" (come). What that means is that a curse does not just land on anybody without a reason. There has to be a cause to bring in the effect of a curse or awaken a generational curse upon a person. There are conditions which empower a curse and without these conditions in place, it must be clearly stated that a curse loses its power as well as its authority to punish and carry out the sentences of judgment. Curses do not operate arbitrarily nor can they be applied capriciously, rather, they derive their power from the authority which they were granted to carry out the sentence of judgment.

> *God has given you authority to cast out all devils and break all spells against your fruitfulness.*

A curse can only operate when the conditions that give it such legal standing are in place; it can only operate when certain conditions are met. Just as blessings are conditional, curses are also subject to certain conditions being in place. However, once those conditions that empower the curse are rescinded, the curses and their consequences cease to have effect.

A curse has no power over the righteous. God has given you authority to cast out all devils and break all spells against your fruitfulness. Balaam's response to Balak when called upon to curse Israel was, "How shall I curse whom God has not cursed? And how shall I denounce whom the Lord has not denounced?" (Num. 23:8). The Bible puts it clearly that the person who remains just and faithful to God cannot come under a curse - "The LORD's curse is on the house of the wicked, but he blesses the home of the righteous" (Prov. 3:33). As a child of God, your home is a blessed home. That is why you should not take it lightly when you see a pattern of strange occurrences in your life and family. However, once the righteous opens the door either through ignorance or willful sinful lifestyle and disobedience to God, the believer can be afflicted or oppressed in some ways which of course may be similar to operationality of a curse. That is why a child of God must know his place in God. Once you appropriate your placement in God, the devil loses his grip against your family.

> ***Once you appropriate your placement in God, the devil loses his grip against your family.***

Factors that bring a curse

There are several factors that cause a curse to work against a person. Some of those factors are:

1. **Sins of the forefathers.** The Bible says "In those days they shall say no more: 'The fathers have eaten sour grapes, and the children's teeth are set on edge" (Jer. 31:29). That presupposes the

possibility of the children suffering the consequences of their fathers' errors. Ask yourself are you a victim of ancestral curse?

2. **Dedication to Satan.** Some people were dedicated to family shrines at birth and so carry the cursed mark of the shrines all through their adult life.

3. **Bringing cursed objects into a home.** Cursed things are what they are – cursed. Once they find their way to your house, they transport the curse to your house. I have seen a situation where a couple could not have babies many years after marriage due to the fact that they had a cursed marriage gift in their home. Once the curse item was revealed and they underwent deliverance, things changed for the better for them and they could have children eventually. That is why I always advice that wedding gifts be seriously prayed over and dedicated to God before use.

4. **Giving honor to demon gods by sacrificing to evil spirits.** This is a practice of making incantations and pouring libations to deities. Such practices

introduce demon spirits to families. They are abominable acts.

5. **Consulting mediums, soothsayers, necromancers and spiritists.** God warned the children of Israel "Do not defile yourselves by turning to mediums or to those who consult the spirits of the dead. I am the LORD your God" (Lev.19:31). He also said to them "As for the person who turns to mediums and to spiritists, to play the harlot after them, I will also set My face against that person and will cut him off from among his people" (Lev. 20:6). God hates such practices.

6. **Iniquities.** This opens the door for curses to invade the life of a person. Iniquity is a graduated sin. When sin has become matured, it becomes iniquity. Iniquity is deliberate wickedness. Examples of iniquities are: a situation where you afflict the poor and the destitute and take advantage of their situation. This can attract a serious curse. Blood sheds, abortions and 'use and dump' attitude can also be classified as iniquity. Don't be a user. Injustice of any kind is iniquity. Some bosses use the labor of people and still shortchange them. No wonder they often become sickly in the later part of

their lives, and their investments lost. Sometimes they withhold wages. These practices invoke curses on an individual. And the Bible speaks against them.

There is also self-inflicted curse. This is a legitimate curse. A "legitimate" curse is when a person deliberately gives himself to Satan and the power of darkness. Legal rights are handed over. Satan is empowered to act, and the curse takes effect. It can only be broken when that handing over is revoked, and the covenant with Satan is specifically renounced. However it takes a total submission to the Lord for curses of any kind to be terminated.

Symptoms of a Curse

Curses can cause:

- Barrenness – not able to have children.
- Sickness – more than 50% of disease is caused by a curse
- Spirit of poverty – financial difficulties – never able to get ahead, defeat, oppression and family breakdown – children on drugs, divorce, separation, etc.

Solution to curses

Jesus is the only solution to the many problems that plague mankind today. He came to destroy the works of the devil over our lives. The whole world lies in wickedness (1 John 5:19), but Christ is the ultimate good that swallows up the wickedness of the world. To be joined with Christ is the essence of true life. Without Him life is just sinking sand. If you are not in Him, you are already under the curse of the law notwithstanding your religious works. And the devil can have a field day practicing his wickedness over your life. But the moment you surrender to Christ, you become a new creature, old things are passed away, (including curses) and all things become new (2 Cor. 5:17). He was made a curse for us as the scripture says – "Christ hath redeemed us from the curse of the law, being made a curse for us: for it is written, Cursed is every one that hangeth on a tree: That the blessing of Abraham might come on the Gentiles through Jesus Christ; that we might receive the promise of the Spirit through faith" (Gals. 3:13-14). This means that we are entitled to generational blessings that flow from God's covenant with Abraham that is activated in all the believers today through faith in Christ. That is what gives us confidence to rebuke the devil whenever we see his operations around us.

The fact that the devil knows that a child of God is not

under a curse will not stop him from attacking. He even tempted Jesus the Christ even when he knew that He is the Son of God and the express image of God. That is why Apostle Paul warned "Lest Satan should get an advantage of us: for we are not ignorant of his devices" (2 Cor. 2:11). This means we must understand the devil's tricks and traps and examine how he uses his key weapons in individually targeted ways to attack each of us. Affliction and oppression are some of the ways he attempts to attack the child of God. We are at war! Satan the devil hates us and wants to destroy us. We must be aware of our enemy's weapons and tactics, because our spiritual life depends on it. Apostle Peter warns also – "Be sober, be vigilant; because your adversary the devil, as a roaring lion, walketh about, seeking whom he may devour" (1 Pet. 5:8). You cannot afford to be a victim. You have to heed Apostle Peter's advice to remain "vigilant". Don't accept any situation contrary to what God has said concerning you. Also don't do things that can activate curses on yourself. Live in the faith of Christ and what He accomplished on the cross for you, and seek to obey the Word of God in all things.

> ***Don't accept any situation contrary to what God has said concerning you.***

May the grace of God keep us all in the faith of Christ in Jesus name.

PRAYER EXERCISE

SCRIPTURE REFERENCE: "Christ hath redeemed us from the curse of the law, being made a curse for us: for it is written, Cursed is every one that hangeth on a tree: That the blessing of Abraham might come on the Gentiles through Jesus Christ; that we might receive the promise of the Spirit through faith." (Gal. 3:13-14)

PRAYER POINTS:

1. Father God I thank you for the gift of Christ, who is the solution to my troubled life in Jesus name.
2. O Lord Jesus, I recognize that without You life is not worth living, therefore I surrender my life and my family to you totally today, come in and take your place in my family and make us new creatures in Jesus name.

3. O Lord my God, I rededicate my life to you, in any way I have attracted curses to my life or family through ignorant or willful acts, I plead for your mercies and forgiveness today in Jesus name.

4. I command every generational curse over my life broken today in Jesus name.

5. I decree all self-inflicted curses, whether legitimate or illegitimate, working against my life and family to be completely terminated today in Jesus name.

6. I command every hand writing working against my progress and the progress of my family to be nullified today in Jesus name

7. I command every door that gave access to satanic affliction and oppression over my life and family closed right now in Jesus name.

8. Father God I pray, in anyway my fruitfulness has been affected as a result of my own foolishness, may the blood of Jesus speak over me today and change my story in Jesus name.

9. I decree fruitfulness over my life by faith in Jesus name.

SPIRITUAL DIRECTION: The couple shall take the communion after praying these prayers before retiring to bed (8th day).

TESTIMONY: 7 years of Barrenness destroyed

Mine was a hopeless case. I was believing God for fruit of the womb for 7 years. I was told I wasn't a candidate for IVF; I had holes in my womb, no eggs, no ovulation.

I met mama Nonnie, She said she didn't believe the doctors report that it is God who has the final say, and declared that I was going to be pregnant. I went home and continued praying. Meanwhile, I heard the testimony of a sister who had been barren for ten years, how she heard a word from the Lord and it became life, so I held unto the word God said through the Pastor that I was going to be pregnant. To God alone be all the glory. 2weeks later I felt sick and I went back to the hospital for a test, it was then confirmed that I am pregnant. God is really faithful!

CHAPTER NINE

ABIDE IN CHRIST

"I am the true vine, and my Father is the husbandman. Every branch in me that beareth not fruit he taketh away: and every branch that beareth fruit, he purgeth it, that it may bring forth more fruit" (Jn. 15:1-2).

One of the ways we deal with the enemies of our fruitfulness is to abide in Christ. To abide in the vine means to hold steadfastly to Christ. And abiding in Christ is the prerequisite to enjoying all-round fruitfulness in life. In as much as we must strive to enjoy all the blessings that are due us in God, we must most importantly stand firm in our relationship with God which of course is the most important thing. Don't go looking for the solution to your unfruitfulness in the wrong places. Such move is the most dangerous move to ever make by couples. There is nothing good you can get from the devil. Whatever one gets from the devil brings in more devils. So if you go to wrong places and use wrong and ungodly means to get children you succeed in initiating your entire family to the devil. You don't want to live in agony of demonic torture all your life, do you? I guess not! So keep off from demon infested food. What we all need in our life is Christ. We must stay glued to Him both in good times and in bad times. He is the hope of glory. He alone gives perfect gifts and does not add sorrow to it.

> ***What we all need in our life is Christ. We must stay glued to Him both in good times and in bad times.***

In the end, eternity is more important than whatever we have or don't have in this brief span of life. It is better to go to heaven childless than burn in hell in an attempt to make babies by all means. So while waiting and battling for that fruitfulness, keep abiding in Christ. He is the solution to the problems we have. Like Job, we must wait till our change comes. And it will surely come in Jesus name.

To abide in Christ means to remain, rest, stay, wait, and continue in Christ. It involves waiting upon the will of God to be done instead of our own will. There is a conflict between the will of man and the will of God. I have heard people say that they don't have the patience of Job and so cannot endure bad situations. You don't need the patience of Job as a believer; what we need is just to abide in Christ. Once our motivation is to please God we would live for Him no matter what may come our way.

Apostle Peter speaks much to encourage those who suffer persecution in any form as believers to keep hope alive; he said: "Yet if anyone suffer as a Christian, let him not be ashamed; but let him glorify God on this behalf. Wherefore let him that suffer according to the will of God commit the keeping of their souls to him in well-doing, as unto a faithful Creator" (1 Pet. 4:16, 19). Peter proceeded to conclude the discourse thus: "But the God of all grace, who hath called us unto his eternal glory by Christ Jesus, after that ye have suffered a while, make you perfect, stablish, strengthen, settle you" (1 Pet. 5:10). What a wonderful promise from God to those who are hurting. You shall be settled in Jesus name. What appears like suffering was just a training process for your settlement. And God has sent me your way at this very moment to push you into that miracle. It is your turning point in Jesus name.

> *Once our motivation is to please God we would live for Him no matter what may come our way.*

Therefore, don't pick up negative attitude towards God or your partner because of the situation you have found yourself. Every problem comes with internal mechanism for self-destruct. So don't let the problem kill your enthusiasm towards Christ. When you abide continually in Christ, you become too hot for the devil to handle. No evil can overcome you because you are connected to Christ. Connection to Him has given us hope of eternal life of bliss with our God. The sense of security in Him emboldens us as we face each day. We have become the apples of God's own eyes. The evil one cannot afflict us or the son of wickedness come near our dwelling. Hallelujah! That is the attitude that puts the devil to shame. I mean a situation where the devil wants to see your tears but sees your joy despite your lack. When he thought he has done his worse to put you down only for you to bubble in the Lord.

Truth is, God is not only interested in providing your heart desires, He much more wants to present you with pride to the world as an example of steadfastness, faith and love for Him. Abiding in Christ is the highest privilege we have been offered. The earlier you appreciate that fact, the better. That is the privilege that even angels peeped to see, yet they are not so privileged.

The question is how do we abide in Christ? Some of the ways we abide are:

1. **We must serve God unconditionally.** Our service to God must not anchor on anything other than God's pleasure. We must seek to pleasure Him the way we seek happiness to ourselves. Unconditional service to God is what frustrates satanic aggression. Once God is your focus, you command the respect of heaven. So keep serving the Lord Joyfully despite your need. He is moved by our love which is epitomized in service. The Bible puts it unambiguously thus: "And ye shall serve the LORD your God, and he shall bless thy bread, and thy water; and I will take sickness away from the midst of thee" (Ex. 23:25). Unfruitfulness is a kind of sickness which can be taken away by quality service. Moses also warned the people, "Because thou servedst not the LORD thy God with joyfulness, and with gladness of heart, for the abundance of all things; Therefore shalt thou serve thine enemies which the LORD shall send against thee, in hunger, and in thirst, and in nakedness, and in want of all things: and he shall put a yoke of

iron upon thy neck, until he have destroyed thee" (Deut. 28:47-48). That shall not be your experience in Jesus name.

> ***Once God is your focus, you command the respect of heaven.***

One of the most potent keys to unlock door of possibility is service. Those who serve are those who operate at the realm of God. God has done the ultimate service to mankind which is redemption. So as we serve Him, we enter into the redemptive grace both for ourselves and for the people we care about. As the blessedness of service attracts God's generosity, the danger of not serving God is grievous as attested to in Deut. 28:47-48. Joshua had to challenge the Israelites on the desirability of serving the Lord. He said to them openly: "And if it seem evil unto you to serve the Lord, choose you this day whom ye will serve; whether the gods which your fathers served that were on the other side of the flood, or the gods of the Amorites, in whose land ye dwell: but as for me and my house, we will serve the Lord" (Josh. 24:15). The moment your mind is made up to serve the Lord continually no matter the enormity of the challenge, the devil loses his grip over you, and God is bound to react favorably towards you too. So service is key. Take hold of it. Peter says we should commit our soul to the Lord in "well-doing" (1 Pet. 4:19).

2. **Love the Lord with all you have got.** You cannot claim to abide in Christ when your love for God is based on what you expect from Him. God is bigger than your expectations, and He can do more than you may ever anticipate. But He wants our love and affection despite our negative situations. Problems have a way of revealing the true character of a person. God wants to know us beyond the facades we wear and sometimes stands aside to watch our reaction when evil strikes like in the case of Job. In the Gospel of John 15:10, Jesus said, "If you keep my commandments, you will abide in my love, just as I have kept my Father's commandments and abide in his love." This therefore shows that to abide in Jesus means to keep his commandments and to keep his commandments means to love God with all your heart and soul and mind and to love your neighbor as yourself (Matthew 22:37–39). One way that we display our love for God is

through our trust, prayer, and devotion to Him. We abide through relationship. We pursue in love. We pray in love. We obey in love. We worship in love. We give in love. We forgive in love. We do everything in love. Until love becomes the basis of our action, we are not different from the devil. The fruit that Jesus speaks of is simply evidence of a relationship with Him. It is a relationship that He initiates through and by His sovereign love. As you seek the things you need from the Lord, let your love for Him overshadow your needs. Love God for who He is, not for what He can do for you. Connectivity with Him in love holds the key to answered prayer. If there is no connection, there is no life, no fruit and we stand the risk of condemnation. He who does not believe (abide) is condemned already because he does not believe in the name of the only begotten Son of God (Jn. 3:18). Through our connection to Christ, we are disconnected from the devil and his works.

Through our connection to Christ, we are disconnected from the devil and his works.

---

3. **We abide in Him through faith**. Faith is a divine currency that accesses the wealth of heaven. It takes faith to serve and love the Lord. Without faith it is impossible to please God. The writer of Hebrews makes the point clearly: "And without faith it is impossible to please God, because anyone who comes to him must believe that he exists and that he rewards those who earnestly seek him" (Heb. 11:6). Faith also implies dependence. The branch is dependent on the vine, but the vine is not dependent on the branch. The branch derives its life and power from the vine. Without the vine, the branch is useless, lifeless, powerless and hopeless. Sap flows from the vine to the branch, supplying it with water, minerals, and nutrients that make it grow. In the same manner, the believer in Christ is completely dependent upon Jesus for everything that counts for fruitfulness. Apart from Him, we can do nothing (Jn. 15: 5). If we can do nothing without Him, it presupposes that we can do all things through Him. You must depend and trust Him for the supplies of your needs according to His riches in glory. Since faith is the basis for asking and receiving, abiding in Him nourishes our faith and enriches our experience with Him. You can never go wrong for trusting the Lord. Faith in Him is the

enhancer of our spiritual stability. Until you depend on Him you cannot advance in your Christian work.

Our God is reliable. He will never leave us or forsake us as we lean totally on Him. Faith also means continuance. "But whoso looketh into the perfect law of liberty, and continueth therein, he being not a forgetful hearer, but a doer of the work, this man shall be blessed in his deed" (Jas. 1:25). This simply means that we go on trusting despite the challenges that confront us each day; that we keep on depending: that we never stop believing. Continuity in Christ is the key to stability in life here on earth and in eternity.

> **Continuity in Christ is the key to stability in life here on earth and in eternity.**

We must do all it takes to remain and continue as the branches. We cannot afford to severe ourselves from the Vine because of setbacks. We are not those who draw back to perdition because of any kind of challenge. We must set our face like the flint and focus continuously on Jesus, the Author and Finisher of our faith. The circumstances of our life do not determine how we relate with Him, His integrity does. The emphasis is in "continuance." We don't just glance at the Perfect Law of Liberty and walk away; we continue therein, not being a forgetful hearer but a doer of the work. If there is anything the devil won't give up, it is trying to stop you from continuing in your faith walk. He is so uncomfortable with our faith because faith puts a check on his activities. Our faith is the victory that overcomes the world (1 Jn. 5:4). So the devil is not after your beauty, but after your faith. Once your faith is intact, your victory is sure. We are more than conquerors as long as we continue steadfastly in our walk with the Lord. Apostle Peter in his thesis told us to continuously grow in our relationship with God. Peter said: "For this very reason, make every effort to add to your faith goodness; and to goodness, knowledge; and to knowledge, self-control; and to self-control, perseverance; and to perseverance, godliness; and to godliness, mutual affection; and to mutual affection, love. For if you possess these qualities in increasing measure, they will keep you from being ineffective and unproductive in your knowledge of our Lord Jesus Christ. But whoever does not have them is nearsighted and blind, forgetting that they have been cleansed from their past sins. Therefore, my brothers and sisters, make every effort to confirm your calling and election. For if you do these things, you will never stumble" (2 Pet. 1:5-10). The Lord will help us in Jesus name – Amen!

PRAYER EXERCISE

SCRIPTURAL REFERENCE: "I am the true vine, and my Father is the husbandman. Every branch in me that beareth not fruit he taketh away: and every branch that beareth fruit, he purgeth it, that it may bring forth more fruit." (John 15:1-2)

PRAYER POINTS:

1. My Father God, thank you for making me a branch knitted to the Vine. I shall be a fruitful branch in Jesus name.

2. Father God, I submit to your pruning in my life and the life of my family, we shall bear much quality fruits in Jesus name.

3. All powers fighting to disengage me from the Vine through challenges of life are terminated today in Jesus name.

4. I decree that by the grace of God, I will abide continually in the Lord. No one shall separate me from the love of God in Jesus name

5. Father Lord, I choose to stay true to you all the days of my life no matter the challenges of life. I shall not turn my back against you no matter what may come my way in Jesus name

6. I submit to the power of the Holy Spirit by faith. My expectation shall not be cut short in Jesus name.

7. I am a fruitful woman/man and my seeds shall be fruitful too in Jesus name.

8. Thank you Father God for answers to prayers in Jesus name I pray – Amen!

SPIRITUAL DIRECTION: Couples shall take the communion after praying these prayers before retiring to bed. (9th day)

TESTIMONY: 23 years of barrenness destroyed

God of WONDERS has visited me! I am 53 years old and I have been married for 23 years with no child. I joined Sisterhood-Africa, was consistent with prayers and Fasting and was led to sow into Mummy Nonnie's Ministry. I sent mummy a message, she replied that God is set to wipe my eyes, I didn't believe it. My period is no longer consistent. Did I mention that I have had over 10 failed IVFs? I thought I had malaria when I became sick... this malaria has turned to Pregnancy. I ran out of the clinic like a mad woman, they had to pursue me to catch me. God is real.... PRAISEeeeeeee the living God, Hallelujah!!!

CHAPTER TEN

REMAIN THANKFUL TO GOD IN ALL THINGS

"Rejoice in the Lord always: and again I say, Rejoice. Let your moderation be known unto all men. The Lord is at hand. Be careful for nothing; but in EVERY THING (empahsis mine) by prayer and supplication with thanksgiving let your requests be made known unto God. And the peace of God, which passeth all understanding, shall keep your hearts and minds through Christ Jesus"
(Phil. 4:6-7).

"Let the word of Christ dwell in you richly, teaching and admonishing one another in all wisdom, singing psalms and hymns and spiritual songs, with thankfulness in your hearts to God. And whatever you do, in word or deed, do everything in the name of the Lord Jesus, giving thanks to God the Father through him"
(Col. 3:16-17).

Approaching God with a thankful heart and a grateful attitude are the sure ways to gain unhindered access into God's presence, escape the rampaging terror of the wicked, and take back what the devil has stolen from us. Thanksgiving is a strong weapon that can invoke the anointing of the Holy Spirit to fight on your behalf. David got this revelation which is why he admonished: "Enter into his gates with thanksgiving, and into his courts with praise: be thankful unto him, and bless his name" (Ps. 100:4). You remember how the Wall of Jericho fell down flat? It was through praises and thanksgiving to God. The moment King Jehoshaphat's army began to sing and extol the name of the Lord there was an ambushment in the camp of the enemy. The enemies of the Jews turned against themselves. Amongst all your prayers, one prayer you must pray is the prayer of thanksgiving. Failure to be thankful to God as a daily devotion is failure along the whole line of life. Ungratefulness to God is a heinous crime.

Thanksgiving is a strong weapon that can invoke the anointing of the Holy Spirit to fight on your behalf.

It is common to see people complain of what God has not done for them, ignoring the things He has done. For whatever lack Satan is taunting you with, look into the matter and you will discover that there is so much that God has done that is greater than what He is yet to do for you. So be grateful always. Joy in the heart equals to answers from God in the hand. When you are grateful and thankful, you attract answers from God. But when you are ungrateful, you shut doors of possibilities against your life.

Ingratitude is a terrible spirit which has the ability to completely ruin the glorious destiny of anybody. But a thankful heart courts God's presence, because God inhabits the praises of His people. To approach the throne of God without thanksgiving is an insult to divinity. If you cannot remember all the good things God has done for you, at least start with the gift of life. You are alive not because you are very careful and smart. There are uncountable smart and diligent people right now lying lifeless at mortuaries around the world. Life is a gift, not a reward. We could not have afforded it if we were to pay for it, otherwise all the rich and great people who are dead and forgotten would be alive today. So don't get used to God, but rather be thankful. Stop complaining about what you don't have rather, pray about them. After praying about them, be thankful. Your case is not as bad as you think. Where you are now may be another person's prayer point. There are parents who wished they had no children considering what evil their children have become – the damage they have caused and the pains they have inflicted on their parents and society. Sometimes, life is so unpredictable and also unfair. But God is not through with you yet. Your fruitfulness is a surety. I know it because God who caused me to write this book at this time has already released grace for fruitfulness to many. Just key into this message by faith and you shall see the glory of the Lord over your life.

> ***When you are grateful and thankful, you attract answers from God. But when you are ungrateful, you shut doors of possibilities against your life.***

Maintain the joy of the Lord

If there is anything the devil is after, it is your faith and your joy. If you let him steal your faith and joy he can get you depressed. And a depressed mind is blind to the goodness of God. Prophet Joel cried out: "The vine is dried up, and the fig tree languisheth; the pomegranate tree, the palm tree also, and the apple tree, even all the trees of the field, are withered: because joy is withered away from the sons of men" (Joel 1:12).

True joy does not depend on the things we have but on the God we know and love. Your love and knowledge of God is the determinant of your attitude towards Him. The absence of joy is the presence of ingratitude. And afflictions abide in the dwelling places of the ungrateful. A person cannot be thankful and not be joyful. Thankfulness attracts joyfulness.

You are a work in progress. You will soon manifest in glory in due time if you faint not. Once you have this understanding about what God is up to in your life, you will come to Him always with a grateful and joyous heart. Paul says, "Rejoice in the Lord always, again I say to you rejoice." I know giving thanks in all circumstances is especially difficult while undergoing suffering. It almost looks like an impossible task to be asked to give thanks in everything. How can we be thankful when there is something that hurts so much? But it has to be done because God commands it. The joy of the Lord is our strength. There is grace from the Lord that turns our mourning into dancing, and sorrow into joy. You must strive to live a grateful life despite your pains. In that way you proof to God that He matters to you more than ten thousand children.

Isaiah 12:3 tells us that it takes joy to draw water from the wells of salvation. Until joy is in place, you cannot draw the water of God's blessing because it can only be found in the place of joy. Any time you appear depressed, you open doors to demonic attacks, but gratitude attracts the joy of the Lord which is your strength. Our love for God is seen in the way and manner we appreciate Him.

Thankfulness attracts God's Favor

Thankfulness can terminate unfruitful existence and launch you into the realm of the miraculous. Many people are putting on a heavy face to protest to God for what they see as unanswered prayers. Someone once said she was going to "tell God the piece of her mind." It made me wonder what level of effrontery. Telling God the piece of your mind does not hurt Him, it hurts you. If you decide to backslide because you are angry at God, that does not change Him from who He is. He is God by Himself and does not need man to validate Him.

Thankfulness can terminate unfruitful existence and launch you into the realm of the miraculous.

Truth is, when you thank Him for the things He has done, you qualify yourself to receive the ones left undone. Joel 1:12 says that "the vine is dried up." What we expected to produce fruit is gone because joy is taken away from the sons of men. Any day you make up your mind to consistently thank God, you are free from the burden of life. Ingratitude is demonic. Some people go about with forlorn look as though they are carrying the whole world on their head. Even Jesus who carried the burden of the whole world was never depressed. The Bible says, "Who for the joy that was set before him endured the cross, despising the shame, and is set down at the right hand of God" (Heb. 12:2).

To go far in life, you must maintain a joyous and grateful disposition towards God. No matter the gravity of the challenge, don't let the devil steal your joy and make you ungrateful. To be ungrateful is to be detained. Hannah only became fruitful when her countenance was no more sad (1Sam. 1:18). Anytime you carry a long face, no matter the abundance of the prayers said over your head, you paralyze the power of that prayer. No matter the weight of the challenge you are going through, still rejoice because joy facilitates divine presence and supply.

To go far in life, you must maintain a joyous and grateful disposition towards God.

Jeremiah 30:19 says, "And out of them shall proceed thanksgiving and the voice of them that make merry: and I will multiply them, and they shall not be few; I will also glorify them, and they shall not be small." A grateful heart is a surety for a gainful life. Thanksgiving delivers fruitfulness. God will set you up for glorification once you are thankful. Whether things are good or bad, always be thankful because thankfulness attracts God's favor.

Thankfulness diminishes your challenge

A grateful heart diminishes the challenge of life and engenders faith to handle the difficulties of life. Apostle Peter said "beloved, think it not strange concerning the fiery trial which is to try you, as though some strange thing happened unto you: But rejoice, inasmuch as ye are partakers of Christ's sufferings; that, when his glory shall be revealed, ye may be glad also with exceeding joy" (1Pet. 4: 12, 13). It doesn't matter what you are going through at the moment, if you can maintain a positive and grateful heart, you will see a way out of that situation.

We can give thanks in the midst of suffering if we have a proper perspective about the Word of God. Suffering is not a death sentence, it's just a setback. It can be a tool to enlarge our faith. The Bible says, "For our light affliction, which is but for a moment, worketh for us a far more exceeding and eternal weight of glory; While we look not at the things which are seen, but at the things which are not seen: for the things which are seen are temporal; but the things which are not seen are eternal" (2 Cor. 4:17–18).

> ***It doesn't matter what you are going through at the moment, if you can maintain a positive and grateful heart, you will see a way out of that situation.***

The suffering we may be experiencing right now is not permanent but the glory that will be revealed in us is eternal. So don't allow bitter experiences to make you embittered, disrespectful and ungrateful to God. Paul asked, "Who shall separate us from the love of God?" then he got a revelation, and responded to his own question: "For I am persuaded, that neither death, nor life, nor angels, nor principalities, nor powers, nor things present, nor things to come, nor height, nor depth, nor any other creature, shall be able to separate us from the love of God, which is in Christ Jesus our Lord" (Rom. 8:35, 38-39).

How to give thanks to God

The first way to show true thanksgiving to God is to always reverence Him in our thoughts, words, and deeds.

Second, we must recognize His deeds in our life. You must appreciate the fact that without Him you can do nothing, but with Him you can do all things through Christ that gives you strength.

Third, we must live in obedience to God. Christianity is not a confession that we make but the life that we live. Your lifestyle is a proof whether you are grateful to God or not.

Fourth, we show gratitude to God for life through the way we treat others. I believe that one of the most profound ways in which we can truly give thanksgiving to God is through serving Him by serving others. Jesus said: "Inasmuch as ye have done it unto one of the least of these my brethren, ye have done it unto me" (Matt. 25:40).

Fifth, we show gratitude to God by being humble.

Humility begets gratitude, while pride begets ingratitude. In the parable of the Pharisee and the publican (Luke 18:9-14), Jesus Christ taught what happens to those who are lifted up in pride and those who are humble. He said: "For every one that exalteth himself shall be abased; and he that humbleth himself shall be exalted."

We must make a choice in the face of adversity whether to gravitate towards God with a grateful heart or move away from Him with an ungrateful attitude. We either react to our afflictions by becoming faithful and thankful or we can become angry and bitter.

My prayer is that the good Lord will grant every one of us a grateful heart in Jesus name.

PRAYER EXERCISE

SCRIPTURAL REFERENCE: "Beloved, think it not strange concerning the fiery trial which is to try you, as though some strange thing happened unto you: But rejoice, inasmuch as ye are partakers of Christ's sufferings; that, when his glory shall be revealed, ye may be glad also with exceeding joy." (1 Pet. 4:12-13)

PRAYER POINTS:

1. Thank you Father God for your love, mercy and favor over my life. I am alive today because of your grace. You have delivered me from the kingdom of darkness and have translated me into the kingdom of your dear Son Jesus Christ. To you be praise for evermore in Jesus name.

2. Thank You my Lord Jesus for the ultimate sacrifice You made for me. Thank You for the gift of salvation. You have set me free and I am free indeed. My household is free because of your eternal sacrifice. Lord I am grateful!

3. Thank You Holy Spirit for your enabling power to live the sanctified life daily to the glory of God. I am grateful for the wisdom to handle the issues of life. It is because of your presence in me that I am not consumed, to you be praise forevermore.

4. Dear Lord, I have made a choice today to maintain a joyous and thankful disposition towards you for the abundance of all things in Jesus name.

5. Thank you Lord because there shall be a performance of the very things you have spoken to me through the pages of this book. To you be glory

and praise, and honor and thanksgiving now and forevermore in Jesus name – Amen!

SPIRITUAL DIRECTION: The couple shall take the communion for the last time after this prayer before retiring to bed (10th day).

TESTIMONY: 9 years of childlessness destroyed

I had been believing God for fruit of the womb for 9 years. I got pregnant through IVF and lost the baby at 7 months, my world stood still. I wanted to take my life. Someone called mummy Nonnie for me and she prayed for me. She told me she saw an angel giving me a blue blanket that by this time the following year, I will carry a baby boy. I felt peace.

This our miracle working God did it! I got pregnant within 3months without IVF. Doctors can't explain it. Our God is awesome. Thank you mummy Nonnie, the oil on your life will not run dry.

MORE TESTIMONIES TO BOOST YOUR FAITH

GOD restored my home and caused me to conceive after 12 years of childlessness

I was married for 12 years, no child. My mother-in-law and sister-in-law convinced my husband to throw my things out. My things were packed and kept at my front door. I ran to Mummy Nonnie, after she prayed for me, she told me that my husband will use his hands and pack my things upstairs by himself and that God will visit me. To the glory of God, my husband packed my things upstairs by himself, and within 2months, I got pregnant for the very first time of my life. Glory be to God

Thank you Jesus. Thank you mummy Nonnie for always standing in the gap for God's children.

13 years of barrenness destroyed

I have been married for 13 years without conception and my marriage was at the verge of collapsing. I have irregular menstrual cycle and I have attempted IVF 6 times without any success.

A sister added me to Sisterhood-Africa early in July and I started typing Amen to every prayer by faith. God bless that sister. After I joined Sisterhood-Africa, I joined the weekly Fasting and Prayers (every Mondays and Fridays), I typed Amen to all the prayers, and I sowed a seed of faith. Before long, I started feeling feverish and I went for test. To my surprise, I was confirmed PREGNANT! God is faithful even in my unfaithfulness. Please help me thank and praise this God, I have never been pregnant in my life. That God will help me carry the pregnancy to full term. Jesus be praise!

My pregnancy test just showed positive!!
It can only be God!!!

I tested because my period is never late.

Where should I start???

I had my first baby 7 years ago, no problems till she was diagnosed with autism. I tried a full year before I became pregnant with the second one who was stillborn at 40 weeks. I cried my eyes out and nine months later, I became pregnant with the 3rd baby who is perfect and now 2 and half years old.

I took in again this January but lost the pregnancy in March. Doctor said hormonal imbalance, poor egg quality, etc. Even my husband was not out of the loop. I have been taking lots of supplements with dedication. My dedication started waning since June. I didn't want to be stressed anymore. If God does not step in, why am I bothering? There will be no results.

Around end of July/beginning of August, someone added me to Sisterhood-Africa. And every day I would scout Mummy Nonnie's Facebook timeline and the SHA group to find prayers. I watched every video and prayed along and believed. I joined the weekly fasting and prayers (every Mondays and Fridays), sowed my seeds and meditated on His goodness. The "August Double Blessings" Facebook live particularly ministered to me. In my spirit, I heard a certain number of sisters watched that video and those were the ones to receive the blessings.

Today, I have evidence of my own blessing. My pregnancy test just showed positive!! It can only be God!!! I know my twin boys are here. God has definitely wiped away my tears because tomorrow would have been hard because it is the 4th anniversary of my son who died at 40 weeks.

Thank you Mummy for saying yes to God.

Thank you for interceding for us.

May God always bless you.

The Testimonies Keep Coming!

1. Mummy, finally the devil has been put to shame! After passing through 11 miscarriages, the Lord blessed me when all hope was lost. I was so fustrated and lacked faith and confidence in God. But in all, He showed me Mercy even when I don't deserve it. God manifested and blessed me and I delivered like the Hebrew women within 20 minutes of active labor. May His name alone be praised!!!

To those who hope in God for this same miracle, I pray that God who change my story and gave me victory, joy and happiness, will locate your homes. You are next to testify in Jesus name Amen.

2. What a miracle working God we have in SHA!!! Mummy, God has done what only him can do, may his name be praise! I return all glory and adoration to Him now and forever Amen.

Mummy, God bless you. I wrote to you two months ago, you replied and told me that my season has come. You also told me that your knees are speaking for me, that you are waiting for my testimony. I sowed my seed and started joining in the SHA fasting and prayers. I also added my friends to SHA because I believe that God is here. Mummy, God has visited me ooo. Because of divine visitation, i went for pregnancy test today, and I tested POSITIVE!!!

Mummy please help me thank God and praise this God for what he has done. That God will help me to carry my twins to full term. For my Sisters on the line, God will visit them too. God bless SHA.

3. Ohhhh my father is real to us in sisterhood-Africa. I was diagnosed of 1cm right ovarian cyst in my scan. I saw a Dr and she told me its usually good when operation is done but I still need to see my Dr to know her thoughts as well. I had an appointment with my doctor and she told me there is no need of doing anything but she needs to get some blood work done and then prescribe clomide cos I have been trying for more than a year. I noticed a lot of changes but I thought its usually like that because I didn't menstruate for close to a year. But God said it is my time!

I went to a store on Sunday and got another pregnancy test kit cos the one I have at home said negative when I first checked. I did 2 tests and it was positive and also the 3rd one. Mummy you are blessed because I told you I want baby as my bday gift and u said it is done. God surprised me with the most precious gift no man can give me.

Thank you mummy. Let ur knees continue to pray for us that all ur preg children won't loss their children and all that seek God face in one way or the other will receive speedily answer. Am 2 months old in this group and I have a testimony already! I join prayer/fasting and also sowed. Thank u mummy for ur listening ear amd eye. I love u mommy.

4. Truly God answers prayers in SHA! I've been trying to conceive for 2years plus now since when my first daughter clocked a year and a half but it proves abortive, I was referred to do series of test which I did and it was confirmed I had Pelvic inflammatory disease and they said with PID chances of getting pregnant is so low, but I didn't allow it get to me and with faith I started typing Amen on every post related to mine, and Lo and behold my sisters I AM PREGNANT... Just like that I didn't even treat the PID but I believe I'm free... I choose to go with God's truth

over doctors fact....

I pray may God in his Infinite mercies bless everyone looking for the fruit of the womb with Twins In Jesus Name. Amen

5. I give God all the glory, no one else could have done this. Mummy, God will continue to bless you and the works of your hands ma. He will increase His anointing upon you and you will do exploits in Jesus Christ's name.

I was invited to the SHA group in August ending and I don't regret it at all. Each time I read testimonies about people getting pregnant, there is a joy that I feel inside knowing that God is in the neighborhood. I sowed and attached my prayer point to it, today I am with my testimony after waiting for almost 3years. Finally, i'm PREGNANT!!!!!!!!!

God is ever faithful and true. I can't even explain the kind of joy and peace I feel right now. Tears of joy can't stop flowing. Thank you so much ma. God who has done this will do for every sister looking unto Him for this kind of blessing in Jesus Christ's mighty name. Amen.

6. Mama Nonnie indeed God is really using you to bless us

in this generation. May God continue to increase His anointing in your life Amen! Someone added me to SHA in July and in the same month I sowed and I sent you a message to help me pray for the fruit of the womb. Mama, God has answered me!!! I tested positive some weeks ago, I am PREGNANT!!!

Miracle working God I bless and appreciate you and for all my sisters believing God for this same blessings, you will testify also.

7. Mummy, I can't keep calm ooooo, I am PREGNANT!!!

I am dancing, my heart is filled with so much joy, indeed there is God in SHA. I messaged u last 2 months that you should pray for me for the fruit of the womb and you replied my mail saying it won't be long, that God wants me closer to Him. I prayed and sowed and the next month, I saw my period. I was sad but I kept trusting God, then I told God that my birthday is coming September 1st that I want God to bless me with the fruit of the womb as my birthday gift. I keyed into the testimonies on the SHA forum, said Amen to prayers, I fasted and prayed and then God ANSWERED!!!

I did the pregnancy test on my birthday morning and it's positive, HALLELUYAH. Thank you Jesus!!! I pray for anyone seeking for the fruit of the womb that my Heavenly Father will visit them right now in Jesus name.

Have faith sisters, God still answers prayers, He will answer your prayers in JESUS name, Amen.

8. I got married in 2013 and I've been trying to conceive. I got pregnant in 2015 but lost the pregnancy. I cried my eyes out that day. Was believing God for another. I waited, fasted, prayed went to churches but nothing happened. In 2016, I went for herbal treatment and I was told I had fibroid. After the local treatment, I went for pelvic scan and there was no fibroid, nothing wrong with my womb.

To the Glory of God, a friend added me to SHA in July. I went through the group and was amazed by the testimonies, then I told myself I will also testify in this forum. I typed Amen to every testimony and prayer point, I fasted every Monday and Friday and I sowed. I missed my period the day I was suppose to see it but was too scared to go for test after 1week nothing came out... Just yesterday I summoned courage, I did home test and got two bold lines. I couldn't believe it so I had to go for blood test, mummy I AM PREGNANT!

I AM Pregnant and I have come to return all the glory to God Almighty. He alone did it!!!

9. JEHOVAH OVERDO HAS DONE IT FOR ME!!!! Mummy God is great, and the TRUE God is indeed in SHA. For four years after delivering my first issue, since then I cannot be able to conceive again. I went to series of test and different treatments but to no avail but last month I sent you, mummy Nonnie a message that I want to be pregnant again and you answered that your knees are speaking for me and I joined the SHA fasting and just two days ago I tested POSITIVE, my God you are great and wonderful glory be to ur name!!! God is in SHA! God bless you mummy Nonnie.

10. Sister Nonny God has done it. GOD HAS DONE IT! Am PREGNANT OOOO!!! I sent you a mail that am trying to conceive and you replied me telling me that God is stepping into my case and HE HAS!!!

I kept on praying and typing Amen to the testimonies and sowed seed of faith in SHA monthly. God is faithful. At a time I gave up hoping but reading the testimonies in SHA encouraged me. I want to also encourage all those believing God for conception that God will answer your prayers. I believe God that with His strength I will carry my baby boys' to full term and deliver like the Hebrew woman. Amen.

God answered me, proved all medical reports wrong, and

saved me money of expenses of drugs and lab. God am grateful. Sister Nonnier I pray God be with you and strengthen you always. Amen.

11. MUMMY OOOO, GOD HAS DONE IT AND I HAVE COME TO SHARE MY TESTIMONY!!!

PREVIOUS PRAYER REQUEST: Good day, mummy Nonnie. May God bless you for the good work you and your crew have been doing in SHA. May your oil never run dry in Jesus name Amen. Ma, please I am here again. I have sow seed, I have prayed, I have typed Amen, and I have cried. But, I promised God, I will never cry again, but, I will always have faith. I only have one prayer request, I pray for God to bless my marriage with the fruit of the womb (twins, a boy and a girl). Please, mummy, help me and talk to God in a language that he will understand. I had a miscarriage by 31st May. People are using style to mock me, but I know the God am serving. Mummy please cry to God on my behalf. My monthly flow is supposed to start next week, but I pray that I will receive a good news of pregnancy before then. I don't want to see it till after 9months when I must have delivered my twins. I am still fasting and praying cos, I know he is a merciful God and your knees are always speaking for me. Thanks and may God continue to enrich your ministry. I believe he has answered my prayers.

TESTIMONY: Mummy Nonnie, May God continue to bless you and may your oil never run dry in Jesus name Amen. I have come to testify for the goodness of the Lord in my life. He is the only God that can do what no man can do. To God be the glory, I was tested positive 2days ago. It can only be God. I want everyone to remember me in prayers so that affliction will never rise again the second time (I had a miscarriage before). I know the God that started this work, will complete and perfect it in Jesus name Amen.

12. Mummy Nonnie please join me thank this your bigger GOD. AM PREGNANT after 6 years of waiting!!

GOD opened my womb last month as my birthday gift cos 6th September was my Birthday after 6 years of waiting. I joined SHA on July. I never believed i'll get pregnant without mummy touching me cos i was told my womb was blocked. I was tired of my situation, i just focused on my phone doing my fasting n typing amen, (like play, like play, e dey work ooo) As the GOD of this great commission has remembered me, i pray that every SHA member that has lost hope of being a mother the GOD of this group will surely locate u, AMEN.

13. Mummy Nonnie I want to appreciate this Wonderful, All Sufficient, Timeless, Way Maker, impossibility Specialist, The Beginning without beginning, The End without an end, Jehovah Overdo, for His Grace, Mercy and Love upon me and my family. Sincerely speaking since someone added me to this wonderful SHA in late July, my prayer life has improved. I always look forward to prayer and fasting days. I keyed into almost all the testimonies of my sisters here believing God for mine. And I also sowed.

I have been believing God for fruits of the womb because I lost my pregnancy baby boy early this year. I JUST CONFIRMED AM PREGNANT. Sisters join me to raise your voice to God that I will carry my pregnancy twins full term. Mummy Nonnie words can't express how grateful am to God for you and this wonderful SHA group. My prayer is, God will continue to Bless, Guide and Direct you and your ministry. He will continue to give you the auction to Function in His vineyard. Amen!

14. Am writing my testimony because I want to encourage most of our sisters who are waiting upon the Lord for the fruit of the womb, please sisters never give up. Always believe that God is up to something (I mean the best) in your Life, honestly is not an easy one at all (being without

a child) but never the less still give God the Glory.........

I got married, stayed for 4years+ without a child it was as if the whole world is crashing on me, BUT I never gave up cos I know that my God liveth and my case must be settled, alot of hospital report and treatment till one day I got fed up. I told my husband that I am going to do it my own way, I remember Sarah that conceived at old age, Hannah nko, what about the dead Lazarus (Talia ku mi) that God must change my story today..... Amen

I went to market bought children things both foot ball, hair packer, we were leaving in two bedrooms apartment then I bought paint that is children colours and paint there room then arrange everything how it should be, write out there names on how it should, that room nobody enters it except my husband, my friends children and I, web my friends come visiting I put food for the children ask them to go inside the room and eat after I will ask them to rub it on my tummy from there we will start praying for them to come, I prayed practically like never before at a time I will forget my own and be praying for my fellow women in the same shoe, And God honored his name in life.....

I conceived but devil came with spotting to the extend the told my husband that I will go for flushing that day I ran made but with hubby's I gave in, but before that I asked them to spare some seconds they agreed, I wept (weeping now) and looked at his cross and told him u answered my prayers and told me it is over (my battle) why must I witness this but never the less u raised from the Lazarus for the death let every dead fetus in the body be raised please protect my baby cos I know that he lives in me, as the flush or wateva I never felt any pain my mind everything was focused on the cross with tear at a time the call me, madam are u OK I say yes cos the are suprise the am not shouting or feeling any pain in fact my mind is not there I don't even know what is happening over, all that is in my mind is " Oh Lord my father, the earth is of u and the fullest there of do not let me to be put in shame cos I trust in U".

One week after the impossible specialist (that is what I call him), Miracle worker proved himself, I started having serious tummy pain with my husband to me to the hospital one our way a voice told that I shouldn't go back to that same hospital that we should go to another one as I was telling my husband thou he refused immediate I sighted anoda clinic along the road because he is arguing I formed as if the pain is unbearable nobody begged him to drive inside the next available clinic, get there the start there test and everything my pain to reduce and immediately send me to scan. Hallelujah

Get to scan I was confirmed 6month pregnant the baby is

perfectly OK, my husband and I fainted, our mouths was open because we don't know what to say, everything was positive, we ran until 10 scan in different places is still the same, my husband couldn't digest it like wise, I was place on drugs, the day of delivery we called almost everyone that we were scared of how it will go like, we didn't inform the new hospital of what we passed thruooo, is just the two of us that knows, as the baby came out my husband ran out and be shouting is a baby oooo, is a baby I was confused I started asking the nurse want is happening I control my emotions because my husband scared me I dnt know what is happening I asked does it have legs, hands, eyes, head, the nurse said yes the baby is OK the brought for me I forgot to ask the sex, all am after is if it is a human, I bless God it was how David my son arrived. After few months God blessed me again with twin girls one is three months older than the sister, and another one after 6 months, my dear it sounds strange BUT God remembers U, he will make you a Wonder, Yahweh is his name............ Hallelujah Amen, Thank you Jesus.

ABOUT THE AUTHOR

Nonnie Roberson is a seasoned spiritual midwife, seer and prophetess; a mother with infectious love who God has trained and prepared for such a time as this. Fondly called "clear eye", a description of the intense prophetic gift upon her life, she is one of the very few endowed with an uncommon prophetic anointing, particularly an UNUSUAL GRACE in the area of fruitfulness and breaking the yokes of barrenness. Through wisdom and the power of the Holy Spirit, she skillfully and delicately unties those who are bound, leading and mentoring God's children with the word of God as they fulfill destiny and take their place in God's end time agenda.

Apart from being a passionate lover of Christ, she is a successful entrepreneur and understands how to navigate the market place ministry. Her ministry reaches out to the poor, outcast and downtrodden in the society. Having pastored a local assembly for 10 years, she has seen the need to reach out to the un-churched. This she does through her outreach programs to prisons, hospitals, prostitutes, drug addicts, widows and orphans.

Prophetess Nonnie Roberson is the founder of Sisterhood Africa (SHA), a closed group of millions of women from all around the globe, who she ministers to and counsels. The group currently has a growth rate of one million new members per month. She is also the founder of the group, Women in Clergy. And she oversees various projects such as **Christ on the Street**, **Detained by Birth** and **Rising Army**.

Nonnie Roberson is married with four biological children and numerous spiritual children.

I trust this book has blessed you in some ways. If so, I'd like to ask you for a favor. Please leave a review about the book on Amazon.

God bless you.

Made in the USA
Lexington, KY
13 October 2017